Letters from Heaven

LETTERS FROM HEAVEN

BY
LILLI KEHLER

COUNTRY VIEW PUBLISHING
ABBOTSFORD, B.C.

Lilli Kehler

LETTERS FROM HEAVEN

c 1995 by Lilli Kehler
  Abbotsford, B.C.

Country View Publishing
#53 - 3902 Latimer St.
Abbotsford, B.C.
V2S 7L5

Canadian Cataloguing in Publication Data

Kehler, Lilli, 1944-
  Letters from Heaven

  ISBN 0-9680260-0-1

  I. Title.
  PS8571.E44L47 1995   C813'.54   C95-911130-1
  PR9199.3K43L47 1995

Printed by Country Graphics, Rosenort, MB

Letters from Heaven

**DEDICATED TO
MY HUSBAND, ERV,
WHO SHARES MY VISION OF HEAVEN,
AND TO
MY DAUGHTER, HOLLY,
WHO LIGHTS UP MY LIFE.**

Letters from Heaven

FOREWORD

In the fall of 1989, a young man appeared in my English class at Trinity Western University. His quiet intensity signaled intelligence and earnest engagement in his work, and perhaps even a little nervousness. It was not long before Jay Kehler became an active and appreciated member of the class.

I had gotten to know his mother, Lilli, sometime earlier since we worked in adjoining offices. Our brief but meaningful conversations told me that she was a more than usually enthusiastic mother of teenagers. Her humorous wit and insightful stories often included interesting moments from their lives.

That Jay and Lilli were good friends was obvious to all of us. The time they shared on our campus, as Jay grew into student leadership, indicated that they were a team reaching into God's service wherever it led them — Lilli, continually cheering on her son, who was heeding God's call by demonstrating maturity beyond his years and developing talents of special order. Jay's being honoured with the university's Citizenship Award in his graduating year was fitting — it was the affirmation of his discipleship and commitment by all who knew him.

The news of Jay's death brought shock and profound disappointment to the university campus. Thoughts of Lilli's sense of loss overwhelmed us. Her courage and bravery were at times

Lilli Kehler

almost too much for us to bear. How joyful it has now been to read the book which tells us the story of a family which is presently separated by realities of time and space but finds its strength in the inexpressible wonder of their son's new life in God's heavenly realms.

I laughed and wept my way through "Letters from Heaven" created from Lilli's imagination and wisdom. This book will certainly bring consolation and comfort to those who grieve and strength to those who mourn. "Letters from Heaven" will inspire readers to faith in a future not bounded by death and loss. It is, indeed, a story of hope and joy!

Professor Lynn Szabo,
Trinity Western University

Letters from Heaven

INTRODUCTION

My son, Jaycen Mark Kehler (Jay), was killed in a motorcycle accident on August 7, 1993 at the age of 21. At the time of his accident he was employed at a summer camp in Sundre, Alberta, as Music and Devotional Leader. He was a strong Christian, very committed to serving the Lord, and influential with his peers.

The week prior to his accident, he had accepted a full time position at Trinity Western University (Langley, B. C.), as Chapel Host. He was to begin his duties there within two or three weeks. He had graduated from Trinity the previous spring with a Business Administration degree. However, his first love was music, and after he graduated, he realized that he wanted music to be more than just a hobby in his life. He wanted it to be, in some fashion, his life's calling. However, God chose to call him home instead, and thus began for us, his family, a time of such excruciating pain and grief that at times we thought it would destroy us. I am employed at Trinity Western University, and thus not only did I have constant, painful reminders of Jay's absence in our home, but also on the university campus where he had been so active and involved for four years. I heard his songs being sung at Chapel, I watched as other musicians played his beloved instruments, and I saw his friends proudly wearing his raggedy T-shirts. I appreciated the mark he had left, but the hole was almost too cavernous to bear at times.

Several weeks after Jay's death, someone (I don't remember who) made the comment that Jay was probably having a wonderful time in heaven, but for our sakes, wouldn't it be comforting if God allowed him to write and let us know how he was doing. "Letters from Heaven" came into existence out of that heart-wrenching longing. It was therapeutic for me to visualize what mischief he might be creating "up there" (being typically Jay), rather than constantly focusing on my own pain and overwhelming sense of loss. I have tried to capture the essence of Jay in these letters — his affable personality, his brash sense of humour, and his love for his family and friends.

I have learned that the grave is a cold, silent place. When I stand at my son's graveside, I am only reminded of the years of separation facing us. Memories don't help much, either. They just make me long and yearn for a period of time that has slipped away forever. Therefore, the only alternative and comfort for me, as a bereaved mother, has been to focus on the reality of heaven and Jay's new and eternal existence. I need to be reminded continuously that my son, so full of life and joy here on earth, has moved on to greater glory. Scripture has assured me that this is so, and I cling to the unfailing promises of God's word.

In the weeks and months following Jay's death, I devoured all the passages relating to heaven found in the Bible. I avidly read every book and pamphlet about heaven that I could lay my hands on. I eagerly listened to stories and songs about heaven. In short, heaven preoccupied my mind and it became increasingly real to me. Strangely enough, four months prior to Jay's death, a couple of his friends produced a video entitled "Goodbye" in which a young

Letters from Heaven

man leaves this world behind and enters into heaven. The video was filmed in the picturesque setting of the "Mission Abby" (Mission, B. C.) and Jay was chosen to play the role of the young man involved. Thus we have in our possession, a video of Jay entering the "gates of heaven". It is a wonderful legacy and another poignant reminder of the reality of his new home.

Towards the end of his final letter from heaven, Jay writes, "Incredible as it sounds, anything and everything that I've been able to describe about heaven falls drastically short of the reality. My humble attempts might be compared to those of a young child who patiently draws a simple picture of his house for his kindergarten friends. He knows, and they know, that there's far more to that house than the drawing shows, but showing them the architect's blueprint would be an exercise in futility. They are too immature and too inexperienced to comprehend the complexities of a professional house design. God's heaven is a very complex place. All I have ever wanted to do was give you a shadowy glimpse of the wonderful home that He has prepared for us. It was never my intention to draw you a blueprint."

Scripture tells us, "No eye has seen, no ear has heard, no mind has conceived what God has prepared for those who love him." (I Corinthians 2: 9)   Nevertheless, heaven has been adequately described in Scripture to give us a tiny preview of what God has prepared for us. It is a place of substance and beauty and harmony, and my embellishment of heaven and its activities can only fall drastically short of the splendid reality. My book was never intended to be a theological dissertation on heaven; it was written to give hope to those whose hearts are breaking, and new vision to those who cannot see beyond today.

My friends, be assured, heaven is as real as the city you are living in and a million times more magnificent. God has prepared it for His children, those who have been bought by the blood of Jesus Christ, and His kingdom will endure forever! Therein lies my hope and comfort, and it is a hope that I want to share with others who are desperately seeking consolation and assurance.

Lilli Kehler

Lilli Kehler

TABLE OF CONTENTS

Letters from Heaven

September 18, 1993
Dear Mom, Dad and Holly,

It has been six weeks since I entered the courts of heaven. Six weeks by earth's standards, that is, because time here is meaningless. I knew you'd be remembering me today, because it is my earthly birthday. Twenty-two years old today! What a child I was when I left! You'd be amazed at my present state of maturity. I don't "see through a glass darkly" anymore.[1] The veil has been lifted and I see and know things beyond your comprehension. (Hey, let me brag just a little, alright?) I'm sure you're all really curious about this place, especially Mom, who always needs to know everything, so I'll try and fill you in as I go along. Some things, of course, need to remain a mystery. Other things are impossible for me to describe in earthly terms. We speak a different language here. It is such a glorious, expressive language. The only thing wrong with it is that it has spoiled me for earthly communication. Everything in earth language now sounds dull and understated. However, since you cannot comprehend our heavenly language, I'll have to paint the picture in terms that you can understand. I want you to catch just a small glimpse of the glory that is heaven.

First of all, I want you to know that I am happy and well. And very much alive! One minute I was lying on a dark Alberta highway,

1

the victim of a tragic accident; the next minute I was being airborne into the sky. For one confused moment I thought I was in a helicopter. Then I realized that I was being held firmly and lovingly in somebody's arms. Awestruck, I gazed around me. We were travelling at lightning speed, but I felt safe and secure in the arms of what I now presumed to be one of God's angels. He didn't speak to me, but his eyes gazed at me warmly and lovingly. Surprisingly, I felt no fear or anxiety. The transition from the highway to the arms of my helicopter-angel was so instantaneous that in retrospect, I am firmly convinced he was standing by, waiting.

We travelled for what appeared to be a very short time, and then came to an abrupt stop. Gently the angel released me. For a brief moment I had the thoughts that a fledgling bird must have when its mother releases it to fly. Would I spiral out of the sky and fall to my death? In the next instant I fully recognized the absurdity of my fear. I could not die again! I had already "passed from death unto life" and was standing at the threshold of the heavenly city. The new Jerusalem!

"Follow me", instructed the angel. Truly a man of few words. I found myself obediently following him, amazed that I was able to keep up. I looked down at my legs. They were moving along rapidly, almost as though propelled by an invisible motor, but in spite of the rapid movement of my legs, I had an eerie sensation of drifting. Motion seemed so effortless. "How is this possible?" I thought. I was to learn later that "prop-drifting" as I came to call it, was a very common way of getting around in heaven, especially if we were travelling long distances. But for now it all felt very new and strange and wonderful.

Our pace slowed somewhat as we approached the gates of the city. The gates were flung wide open, and the angel and I joined the throngs of people that were slowly passing through. There were so many people, and yet there was no crowding, no pushing, no shoving. I took my time and closely examined the "pearly gates". I don't know much about gems, but this had to be the real thing. I've never seen pearls with a rosy sheen to them, but these gates had a rosy glow that could only be termed as "other-worldly".   Incidentally, I'm not colour blind any more, so I notice these things. Too bad I don't need to wear socks in heaven; now I could match them up.

Having passed through the gates, I continued to follow the angel. We had temporarily abandoned the prop-drifting and were walking at a more leisurely pace. I came to a startled halt as I felt the texture of the street beneath my feet. It felt smooth and glassy and it gleamed brightly. The golden streets of heaven! They really existed. It occurred to me standing there that although I had never doubted the Word of God, yet my finite, earthly mind had never been able to truly grasp the concept of golden streets. Golden rings, yes. Golden ornaments, yes. But miles of golden streets? The angel looked alternately amused and impatient as I kept bending over to stroke the pavement. He had seen it all before, and I was delaying him. I used to admire your gold stamp collection, Dad, and hoped that someday I would inherit it. Now I've inherited whole streets of gold instead.

Lilli Kehler

Impatient with my tardiness, my angel guide began to prop-drift again. In spite of our rapid pace, I managed to catch glimpses of homes along the way. They were well set back from the boulevard and surrounded by lush trees and shrubs. The lawns were neatly trimmed, but unlike those on earth, they were studded with flowers. In fact, it was difficult to separate the grass from the flowers, so my initial impression was that the yards looked like those jewel-coloured Indian carpets that Mom always raves about. I didn't notice any cats or dogs running around the yards, but that's not to say there aren't any. I'll check on that before I write again, okay? I'm sure Holly is anxious to know if there are cats in heaven.

As I mentioned earlier, the angel wasn't much of a talker, so my thoughts were my own. For some reason, I suddenly remembered that silly story about the society lady who expected a large mansion in heaven and to her chagrin was given a very modest home. The word was, she "hadn't sent much on ahead!" Since I had been a struggling student for so many years, I hadn't sent much on ahead either. My expectations were not high. However, suddenly, my angel guide stopped in front of a surprisingly substantial home with tall marble columns and a wide wrap-around verandah. "Yours!" he said. "Mine?" I asked in astonishment. "How can this be mine? I never earned very much, and I only had such a short time on earth to tithe." Swinging the big glass doors open in front of me, he grunted with characteristic economy of speech, "You gave faithfully of the little you had." I got the picture.

The interior of my home is beautiful. Satiny hardwood floors, cream coloured walls and marble counter tops. The kitchen is spacious and bright, but there is no refrigerator and no stove. We obviously don't need to prepare and store food in earthly fashion. There is very little furniture in the house. The angel told me that when I get around to it, I can shop for my own furniture. Exactly what it means to "shop" in heaven, I will have to discover. In the hallway as you come in, there is a beautiful, green occasional table. As I said earlier, I don't know much about gems, but I'm sure this table is genuine emerald. Can you imagine owning a whole emerald table on earth? The table held a cream coloured vase with freshly cut roses. Fragrant and beautiful! Because emerald is your birthstone, the table will always remind me of you, Holly. There are no light fixtures in my house, and no built-in vacuum system. And why should there be when Jesus is the light and nothing in heaven becomes "defiled and corrupted." In lay language, guys, no more dust and dirt. How refreshing!

It's important to mention that the nagging pain in my elbow has completely disappeared, and I haven't had one migraine since I arrived here. Maybe that's because I haven't had any all-night study sessions lately. Speaking of "night", there isn't any. No nights, no darkness. There are only varying degrees of light, ranging from brilliant, white radiance to softest twilight. The air is clear and fresh and has a sharp, clean taste. I wish I could send you some. I recall earth people's preoccupation with physical fitness and eternal youthfulness. This air is definitely an elixir, but unfortunately, it can't be bottled.

Lilli Kehler

I'm jumping around from topic to topic, but there is so much to tell you that I'm having a difficult time sorting it all out. However, I know you must be anxious to hear about Grandpa and Oma. I ran into both of them almost as soon as I got here. Or perhaps I should say they ran into me. It was almost as though they knew I was coming and were waiting for me. It took me a minute to recognize them. I was so young when Grandpa went to heaven that I didn't have a clear picture in my mind of what he looked like, but when he introduced himself to me and gave me a big hug, there was an instant sense of affinity. He was distinctly "family". I haven't looked into a mirror lately, but I think we have the exact same colour of eyes, those "blue, blue Kehler eyes" as Mom always used to call them.   But the really big surprise was Oma! Oma was not the withered, senile old lady that I remembered from the care home. This Oma was tall and strong-looking, with very dark, curly hair. I couldn't believe her laugh. It's almost as bad as Mom's. She's an amazing guitarist, and we've played together several times. Now I know you're wondering how that's possible. Our taste in music on earth was very different, but that's another thing that's so hard to describe. The music up here just "meshes".   Individual taste in music blends together and creates a new sound altogether, one that is achingly beautiful.

I could go on and on about the people I've met up here. Danny and Kirsten and I have had some interesting talks, although "talks" isn't an exact description of the process up here. There were no tongues wagging and no mouths moving, nevertheless, we "talked". Oh, and before I forget, you'll be interested to know that along with

Letters from Heaven

Grandpa and Oma, I have visited with my formerly unknown sibling. That's the one that went to heaven without ever experiencing earth. I know you're dying to know whether it's a he or a she, but you'll just have to wait and see for yourself. He/she doesn't feel he/she missed a thing by never having been officially born. Eternity began before birth. Doesn't that sound weird and wonderful?

I've also met a few of the Bible characters. Awesome people, although quite intimidating. Many of them took such risks in their earthly life. My biggest risk was singing and playing in front of an audience. Hardly comparable! I think my favourite character so far is David, probably because he is a musician. I never think of him as a former king. He's just a cool, ordinary guy that I can discuss music with.

Lest you think that all I do is sit around and play the guitar, that's not so. A group of us took a long hike along the River of Life recently. We don't always prop-drift. Sometimes it's fun just to walk the normal earth way, especially if we're not in a rush. The scenery was breathtaking; better than Mount Baker in the autumn. The water in the river appeared crystal clear and cool. No pollution here, remember. None of us became thirsty in spite of the long hike, but the water looked so fresh and inviting, that we couldn't resist having a drink. Holly, none of that bottled stuff that you and I were always "guzzling" down there even remotely compares. As for you, Mom and Dad, just imagine what the coffee will taste like made with that water. Espresso supreme! Incidentally, I haven't noticed any coffee shops around here, but then, I haven't been looking. When I get some time, I'll check things out and let you know what the score is. I haven't forgotten your penchant for coffee shops.

Back to our hike, we also thoroughly enjoyed the "picnic lunch" that we picked from the trees along the river. How can I describe that fruit? One looked and tasted something like a fresh, juicy peach. Another one, surprisingly, tasted almost like a freshly baked loaf of bread. We returned from our long hike late in the day, but instead of feeling exhausted and sore, we felt surprisingly refreshed and energetic. One of your famous foot-rubs would have been nice though, Dad, just for fun. Save them up for me, okay?

I have left the best for last. The angel allowed me to admire my new home for a little while, and then urged me once again to follow Him. "More important things to do," was his brief reply when I asked him what was happening. I realized just how important, when he led me back along the street, prop-drifting once again with amazing speed, right down to the lake. The lake I'm talking about is the crystal-like sea referred to in Scripture. It is located at the centre of the city, and lies in shimmering, glassy splendour right before the throne of God. I wanted to stop and gaze in awe around me, but my angel guide kept propelling me forward.

And then I saw Him, walking towards me from the other side of the lake. I had no difficulty in ascertaining who He was, because He walked toward me encompassed in brilliant, white light. Mom, Dad, Holly... I met Jesus Christ in person! Now, this is where words really fail me. Picture this if you will. Here I am, an ordinary "geek" just arrived from lowly planet earth. My initial state of euphoria has evaporated, and for the last few hours I have been experiencing a full gamut of emotions. Irrepressible joy, certainly, but also a little earth-nostalgia, a hint of fear, and more than a little confusion. Suddenly I am enfolded in a set of arms so powerful and loving that without a doubt, I know I am in the presence of the Son of God. His love and His peace surround me like a warm, fragrant cloak and I know that I have come home! As he hugs me, I hear the words, "Well done, my good and faithful servant." I look around curiously to see if Billy Graham has suddenly arrived as well, and then I realize it is me He is speaking to. Me! I couldn't believe it. What had I ever done to deserve this kind of tribute? And then I realized, of course, that I had done very little. In fact, Jesus Christ had done it all for me. He paid the penalty on the cross for my sins. To my credit was the fact that I knew I was a sinner and in need of salvation. I accepted Him as my personal Saviour and Lord, and this was my reward. How amazing! A new song of praise began to well up within me, and I knew that I was on the verge of my greatest musical composition. How easy it is to be creative, when the object of all my praise, my blessed Saviour and Redeemer is standing right there before me, holding my hands in His nail-scarred ones, loving me with an everlasting love. What an indescribable moment!

I believe this is enough for my first letter. Don't worry, there will be more. Perhaps not as lengthy as this one, but I will stay in touch. I know what my family is like about celebrations such as birthdays, Thanksgiving and Christmas. Here, life is an ongoing celebration. There, you're so bound by occasions. So, you'll hear from me from time to time. In the meantime, I know you miss me. How could you not? (I'm such a great guy!) But, please don't let my absence rob you of all joy. Weep if you must, but please don't weep for me. I have joy now such as I've never known before. You must never forget the promise of Scripture: "There are three things that remain — faith, hope, and love — and the greatest of these is love."[2] My love for you and your love for me is a reflection of God's love for us, and it can <u>never</u> die. Don't let your life come to a halt because I'm no longer there. God is still in His heaven, and I'm right here with Him, waiting, as you are, for that ultimate, joyful reunion. However, until that great day arrives, carry on with the tasks God has given you and lean upon Him. He will uphold you with His mighty arms. I have seen those arms, my dear family, and they're adequate for the task.

Love, Jay

Letters from Heaven

October 11, 1993
Hi, My Family!

Thanksgiving Day today. A special day on earth and a very special day in heaven. It is a special day in heaven because the angels rejoice when they hear all the praise and thanks to God emanating from your planet. Many days they hear nothing but grumbling and complaints!

Last year around our Thanksgiving table, Dad asked each of us to share what we were thankful for. I distinctly remember mentioning my family, my friends, our nice home, and above all, my relationship with Jesus Christ. Who, except God, knew that this year I would be separated from my family, my friends and my earthly home? However, not from Jesus Christ. Scripture confirms that, "nothing ever separates us from the love of God that is in Christ Jesus."[3] In these last couple of months, I have experienced the love of Christ in a marvellous new way. The old gospel hymn writers used to call it "a divine fellowship", but until I arrived here, I didn't fully understand that term. Now, I know! And, as far as the separation from my family and friends is concerned, let me remind you once again that it is definitely short-term. So, be happy for me as I grow in knowledge and wisdom. You'll all catch up eventually.

Lilli Kehler

I presume you're having some of my student friends in for Thanksgiving dinner again. Tradition demands it, of course. With a little bit of luck, nobody will complain about the raisins in the dressing this year! I am happy to report that there are no raisins in heaven. Fresh, juicy grapes in abundance, but no dried up, wrinkled, raisins. I have always maintained, and of course now I know, that raisins are the product of an imperfect world where things wither, decay and rust. Here, the grapes stay plump and fresh on the vine.

Speaking of Thanksgiving dinner, I must share that I have had some royal feasts since I arrived here. Actual hunger is an earth-sensation that no longer victimizes us, but we eat for pleasure and for fellowship. Food is readily available everywhere; the trees are laden with fruit and vegetable gardens abound. Generally speaking, everything is completely and deliciously edible in its natural state, and this is how I prefer it. However, I have noticed some "die-hards" around who seem to prefer their food cooked. The cooking process up here is not done on typical earth stoves. The heating devices used remind me somewhat of earthly hot plates. When you want something heated or cooked, you just flick on a switch and the device instantly begins to heat. It's not plugged in anywhere, it just seems to derive its energy from the air. If you think that sounds absurd, remember what this air does for the body. It's all quite miraculous, and why not? This is heaven. In future letters, I will also describe some other forms of "cooking". (After all, what would heaven be without corn roasts and fish fries?) The fruit and vegetables taste considerably different from those I consumed on earth, partially because there's far more variety and partially because heaven's soil and air are entirely pure. Organic growth at its finest. Considering as well that my taste buds, along with my vision and hearing, have never been so well developed, you can well imagine the delight that food is. On the other hand, we never over-eat, and we never gain weight.

I spoke about fellowship. I have had a few guests in my home, and have been invited out quite frequently. Last month I mentioned my budding friendship with David. One night David invited me to his home for a fellowship evening. I had a wonderful time, but the guest list read like a prestigious Who's Who of the Bible elite. Moses and Aaron were there, along with their sister Miriam. David's friend Jonathan was there and they are still good buddies. In heaven we are all equal, but whenever I meet these Bible characters I always feel a sense of awe. Understandable perhaps, in light of the fact that I grew up on stories of their extraordinary feats. We "johnny-come-latelys" of the technological era had some very bold and courageous role models to live up to.

Going from patriarchs to pets, I did make some discoveries about the feline population in heaven, Holly. In the process of taking a solitary walk along the River of Life one day, I noticed an enchanting, grassy footpath leading off to the right. Curiously, I followed it. After some time of walking leisurely, I began to prop-drift. Heaven's wonderful fast gear! It was a worthwhile trip. Suddenly, grassy meadows unrolled before me like a waving, green carpet, studded with flowers of every colour and type. Dad, I can just see you with your Reader's Digest Gardening Manual in hand, trying to identify all these flowers. You would have a ball! Away off in the distance near some low, blue foothills, I saw horses galloping around. A few had riders on them, but most of them were just frolicking around on their own.

To the west of this scene, I saw a herd of sheep contentedly grazing in a lush green pasture. Fluffy, white lambs butted against each other at a nearby shallow pool of water. They were incredibly cute. Slinking in and around the sheep and lambs were a couple of magnificent looking lions. For a split second I felt alarmed, and then I saw Biblical prophecy fulfilled right before my eyes. One of the little lambs butted against that huge lion daringly; the mouse teasing the cat, as it were. The lion blinked in astonishment, and then gave the lamb a friendly cuff with his great paw. The lion must have thought he was a pussy-cat; he underestimated his own strength. The little lamb sprawled over, its legs askew. The lion gave the lamb a puzzled lick, and when there was no response, he lay down beside the lamb and pulled it towards his huge chest. The lamb nestled there like a baby against its mother's breast. Unbelievable! However, I am meandering. Near some low, leafy bushes on the other side of the pond, I saw an assortment of cats. Small cats, large cats, short-haired cats, and long-haired cats. I wandered over and began to harass them! (In a nice way, of course). One rather obese, gray and white cat reminded me somewhat of our Jingles. She was lazily stretched out under a bush, purring loudly, watching a bright orange butterfly with one eye. The other eye was closed. I tried to tease her into playing, but this kitty wasn't in the mood. If you can't lick 'em, join 'em, right? I lay down under the same bush, put her on my chest and dozed for awhile. Our bodies don't require sleep, of course, but "cat-naps" are refreshing.

I learned when I got back to heaven proper that animals have been given their own special domain. People are free to visit this vast "animal park" anytime and enjoy the animals. Some folks spend a lot of time over there; others have relatively little interest. I enjoyed it tremendously. It was a quiet, restful place. Next time I'll take my guitar along and entertain the animals. I believe they'll be a most discerning audience!

I haven't even begun to explore the riches of heaven. There are wide, golden boulevards intersecting the main street that I haven't checked out yet. I have also noticed a number of narrow, cobblestone roads forking off from these boulevards. They look quaint and intriguing. I want to explore all the grassy footpaths and trails that I've seen, as well. I have been told by people that have been here for ages (literally) that even they haven't begun to see all there is to see, and to do all there is to do. There are great vistas to explore. I'll be taking you on one grand sight-seeing tour when you get here!

One of the most enjoyable things about heaven is its people. Lest you think that we are a bunch of "spirit clones" up here, let me straighten you out. People have bodies and faces and features and hair. Each person is as unique as they were on earth; however, here they are at their absolute best. To illustrate, think for a moment of some person that you know well and love dearly. Other people may see thin, stringy hair, blemished skin, and heavy hips, but you see

15

sparkling blue eyes, long, graceful legs, and a generous, winsome smile. That's heaven. Everyone sees everyone else at their very best. People see each other through the eyes of Jesus and through the eyes of love. I still look like me, and certainly you'll recognize me when you get here. However, to describe it in earthly language, my blue eyes appear even bluer, my skin is unblemished and my hair has golden highlights in it. Those little "handles" at my waist that always annoyed me, are gone. And Mom, you will be so pleased to know that I don't chew my fingernails anymore. This all conforms to my earlier description of Oma. There's just no comparison to the stooped, white haired old lady in the care home. There's probably not even any comparison to the young, healthy woman she was earlier in her life. Her dark, curly hair is so shiny and springy, she has very mischievous blue-gray eyes, and her laugh entertains everybody around her. Heaven is a place of strengths, and each of our strengths are exhibited to the fullest. This does not only apply to our appearance, but also to our personalities and to our gifts and talents. Heavenly people are unique, attractive people who for the first time ever, are living up to their full potential.

Let me paint a futuristic picture of Holly to illustrate my point. She's not a bad looking "chick" by earthly standards, but when she gets to heaven, she won't need the make up, the curling iron, or the eye prosthesis. Her hair will never have split ends, her eyelashes will be long and luxurious without mascara, she will have smooth, glowing skin and two gorgeous blue-gray eyes, both sighted. Her already bubbly, outgoing personality will be new and improved, because there won't be any fears or tears underneath. Practicing scales on the piano will be a thing of the past, because her artistic ability will have reached its full potential. She will not only be playing masterpieces, but composing them.

Speaking of pianos, I have to tell you that the first piece of furniture I "shopped" for in heaven was a piano. As you can well imagine, we have some amazing craftsmen here, and making a choice was quite the challenge. I eventually claimed a shiny, black baby grand. I say "claimed", because we don't actually purchase anything here. We just go and pick it out and take it home. Heaven works on a strange kind of barter system that I will have to describe to you sometime in greater detail. For now, shall we say I received a beautiful piano in exchange for some free labour and some original pieces of music which I wrote for the guy's daughter. He loved creating the piano, and I loved creating the music. In a future letter, I must also describe some other items of furniture that I "claimed" for my home. I have developed a fascinating colour scheme. Not Mom's taste, that's for sure, but I like it! I promise I won't try and decorate her mansion before she gets here! Another good thing about heaven is that we don't need furniture vans to move furniture around. I just picked the items up, placed them on my back and prop-drifted home. We are not only unique, attractive people; we have the strength of Samson (and then some!). It's a great asset to have.

I must break away, once again. In closing though, I would like to tell you that the angels here are God's servants, and because they are God's servants, they are also (in a way) our servants. You see, we are the children of God, and thus are privy to his riches. To make my point quickly, it seems that in my new "princely" role, I am able to request special guardian angels for each of you. I have done this, and all three of you are now being carefully watched over by the guardian angels assigned to you. Not much slips by them, so consider yourselves in safe, competent hands. Remember that the next time you go for your driver's test, Holly. You'll do good!

I'll write again soon. Other occasions are right around the corner.

All my love, Jay

Letters from Heaven

November 11, 1993
Dear Holly, Dad and Mom,

You'll notice I changed the order of the salutation this time. I didn't want you to think that I'm playing favourites. So, my family in random order, this will be a brief letter.

It is Remembrance Day today, a day that has, in the past, been largely ignored by the Kehler family. However, it is a day of commemoration on earth for the fallen of two wars, and although I did not fall in a war, I knew you'd be remembering me for the simple reason that, like all those fallen soldiers, I am no longer with you. All I really remember about past Remembrance Days is that Dad never failed to wear a poppy in his lapel. I guess he thought he looked good in red.

I have met many veterans here in heaven, veterans from numerous wars. They still sit around and swap war stories, but the talk is not of violence and bloodshed. Physical and mental wounds have healed, maimed limbs have been restored, and bonds have been formed between veterans of all nations. The old timers are fascinated by the descriptions of the modern weaponry being used in more recent wars. My good friend David is still convinced there's nothing like the sling shot. He target practices all the time (for what

I don't know), and he really is very good. He's been trying to teach me to use the sling shot, but I can't get the hang of it. I keep teasing him that there are no more Goliaths to slay, so let's drop it! Now, when it comes to archery, I give him a run for his money. As you can see, there is competition in heaven — but no poor sports!

The only war I really remember is "Desert Storm", the Gulf War, and I wasn't involved in that. However, I do remember a couple of "wars" I was involved in — at home. (Or is that stretching it a bit?) Do you remember the time that Dad washed my mouth out with soap? That was war! I suppose Dad won that war because I decided swearing wasn't a worthwhile endeavour. Do you remember the time I ran away from home? Do you still have my goodbye note? I know you kept it. You thought it was funny. Poor little me. Dad was out of town that week, Mom was in a bad mood, and nothing seemed to be going right. I really felt I had no choice but to leave a home where I wasn't suitably appreciated. I packed a bag with some cookies and a drink, and hid in the bushes along the creek back of our house. I thought Mom would come looking for me, and it made me very angry when I saw her playing outside with Holly, seemingly unconcerned by my absence. The afternoon dragged on, and I was getting very tired of my own company — and that of the mosquitoes — but I was determined to make you all suffer. Just as my stomach started to rumble complainingly, I heard Mom say in her loudest voice, "Hey, Holly, it's almost supper time. Go inside and get your jacket, and we'll go to MacDonald's for a hamburger." You'd think Holly would refuse. I mean, what decent little sister could think about MacDonald's when her brother was missing?

Letters from Heaven

Instead, she pulled her jacket on within two minutes. I could see her through the kitchen window as I glumly contemplated my options. Revenge is sweet, but supper at MacDonald's was not a nightly occurrence. Sometimes one just had to put one's pride aside and review what was really important. For some reason or other, Mom didn't look too surprised to see me coming out of the bushes a few minutes later. And MacDonald's hamburgers were exceptionally good that night. Memories, memories...!

I am continuing my studies — after a fashion. I know you think that being in heaven, I should know it all. Not true. If I knew everything, I would have the knowledge of God and that isn't possible. And so, I continue to learn. As you can well imagine, we have some top-notch lecturers here representing all faculties — the sciences, mathematics, theology, music, business, history, and many more. The only subjects we don't have are the languages, for obvious reasons. We all understand each other perfectly up here. There is a universal language "spoken" in heaven and as I mentioned in an earlier letter, it is far superior to any language ever spoken on earth.

I know exactly what's going on in your mind right about now. If we're perfect in heaven, why is there a need to further our education? Let me explain. First of all, may I remind you that "perfect" is an earthly term, and heavenly people don't necessarily fit into slots designed by mortals. Secondly, and I remember this all too well, earthly people often pursue their studies only as a means to an end. They try to excel in order to achieve awards, monetary gifts and recognition. Here in heaven, the process of gaining knowledge and wisdom is an end in itself. It is pure pleasure to sit at the feet of Jesus and have him explain the New Testament parables in person. No offence to Dr. Evans, whom I learned much from, but I am now taking instruction from "the Master." It is a wonderful experience to wander into the class of some great historian, and learn how everything in heaven and on earth has fitted together from the beginning of time. In addition to Jesus, whose classrooms are always understandably filled, there are many superior instructors - some whose names I recognize from my former history books - others whom I've never heard of before. I tend to avoid the business classes. I suppose I had enough of them at Trinity Western. I still don't understand what prompted me to study business. I learned quickly that being a Math whiz does not automatically make one a prime candidate for entrepreneurial pursuits. Mom, do you remember me teasing you, telling you on several occasions that I needed that business degree in order to administer the "millions" I was going to earn as a musician and song writer? I'll always remember the frightened look that flashed across your face. I could never figure out what you were afraid of — my being a musician, or my being rich. (Maybe both!) As it is, I am now a musician, and I certainly am rich. At least, my father is! "My father is rich, with houses and land." Do you remember that old song? Management is a necessary concern, even in heaven, but there are others interested and willing to pursue it, so I'll leave it to them. The beauty of this place is in its choices! Earth has its choices, too, but we don't always have the wisdom to make the right ones.

On another subject altogether, a group of us went for another long hike the other day. Not along the River of Life this time, but down one of those cobblestone roads that I was telling you about in my last letter. It was a cooler day than usual, and I found myself enjoying the slight autumnal tang in the air. We had a great time, talking and laughing and singing. As I looked around at the group I was with, I realized I was spending more and more time with this particular group of people. Everybody gets along well with everyone else up here, but I guess I like the people in this group because most of them enjoy music and seem to have the same zany sense of humour that I do. There are some people, even in this paradise of a place, who don't relate to my sense of humour. Some of them wouldn't appreciate your bad jokes, either, Dad, so be forewarned. You might just have to bring Mom along if you want somebody to laugh at them!

We changed our pace after awhile and began to prop-drift. We can cover enormous distances very rapidly by this method of travelling. In no time at all, we found ourselves in the vicinity of a range of towering, snow-capped mountains. It was the first time I had seen snow in heaven. The scenery, as always, was stunning. As we came closer, we saw ant-like figures crawling along the mountain side. One of the guys with us gasped with delight. "Mountain climbers", he exclaimed joyously. "I've always wanted to try this, but we never lived near the mountains, and I never had the time or the money to pursue it." We watched for awhile, as the ant-like figures climbed higher and higher. They were obviously having a race to see who could get to the top first. I saw no mountain climbing gear such as is commonly used on earth; these guys were climbing unassisted. A couple of the guys from our group went off to join the climbers. The rest of us opted to prop-drift up, instead. Much easier. When we arrived at the top, we looked around us in wonder and amazement. I have never, not even in heaven, seen a view like this. Thousands of feet below us lay a rich, green valley, somewhat similar to my animal park. However, this valley was inhabited by people. A long, winding river frothed and foamed its way through the entire length of the valley. Along its banks were spacious farm homes, each surrounded by its own copse of trees. Lush orchards and gardens stretched out behind the homes. Annette, one of the girls in the group, took the words right out of my mouth: "Country living at its finest," she breathed. "God has made such marvellous provision for the folks that have always preferred the wide open spaces." I wondered then how many more surprises God would have in store for us in this beautiful, heavenly land. We decided to leave the exploration of that valley for another day and skied down the mountainside with some skis that had been left in a nearby storage shed. You can tell my friend, Colin, that I skied more proficiently than I ever did on earth. Tell him that by the time he gets here, I'll be skiing circles around him. I enjoyed the exercise, and the fresh mountain air was exhilarating. We worked up quite an appetite, and when we got down to the bottom, we were invited to join our mountain climbing friends for a corn roast. What a feast, and what a perfect day! As always!

This was going to be a brief letter! In closing, let me tell you that I am aware that Christmas is just around the corner. I also know that this will be an unusually difficult time for you, my family, because I'm not there to share it with you. We've always made such a "big deal" of Christmas; being together as a family, celebrating the Christmas traditions, buying and opening the gifts. Maybe this year you need to concentrate more on Who the celebration is actually for. Here in heaven we are celebrating the amazing fact that Christ lowered Himself to go to the earth and become human. It is only since I have arrived here and seen what heaven is like that I can fully appreciate the sacrifice He made in leaving heaven to live amongst men. Much as I love you, I wouldn't want to do that. That says something about the calibre of His love, doesn't it? I realize Christmas is a time for families, but concentrate on the fact that our family will be together for all eternity. One Christmas at a time, folks! I don't want to become the central figure of your Christmas this year by my absence. Jesus holds that position by the power of His presence. Enjoy <u>Him</u> this Christmas!

Lots of love, Jay

Lilli Kehler

December 25, 1993
Dear Dad, Mom & Holly,

Special Christmas greetings to the three of you. Christmas is a special celebration — in heaven and on earth — however, as I mentioned in my last letter, we celebrate the occasion from a slightly different perspective than you do. You celebrate the fact that Jesus Christ came to earth; we celebrate the fact that He returned to heaven. The thirty-three years He spent on earth was such a sacrifice for Him, culminating in the sacrifice of all sacrifices — His death on the cross! However, because of that great sacrifice, I am here, enjoying eternal life, and you are there, anticipating the joys that are yet to come. It is not my intention to make you envious, but heaven is an enviable reality! When my friend, Danny, was killed in an airplane crash several years ago, I remember trying to visualize what heaven might be like. Now I'm in a position to know, and I must admit that my imagination fell very short of the real thing. As scripture puts it: "No eye has seen, no ear has heard, no mind has conceived what God has prepared for those who love him".[4] Therefore, be aware that because I have my restrictions, and you have your limitations, the picture of heaven that will emerge in my letters to you is only a vague, watery reflection of the real thing. However, one can but try, especially in light of the fact that the three of you are always so inquisitive!

26

Letters from Heaven

I wonder what your Christmas was like this year? I have a feeling that you made some drastic changes. Christmas Eve was always our exclusive family time, and Mom never let anything interfere with that. The evening usually began with an early dinner, then the Christmas Eve carol service at church, and then home to open the gifts. Naturally, Mom and Dad always found some unique ways to procrastinate the gift-opening process. The Christmas story always had to be read, in full. Then we would all share some thoughts and insights on Christmas, followed by a prayer time. Holly and I kept our prayers short, but Mom and Dad had a way of dragging everything out. We (Holly and I) suggested year after year that we do all those things after the gifts were opened, but Mom and Dad never complied. (Perhaps a tinge of sadism?) After all that, Christmas Day was always a bit anti-climactic. Knowing you as I do, I suspect that you did not spend Christmas Eve alone this year. You probably had friends and relatives in, and tried to make the evening as busy as possible. And no doubt, you also surrounded yourselves with people on Christmas Day, and once again, kept yourselves too busy to think. You had a big 5 ft. 9 inch, 155 lb. vacuum to fill, and I'm sure it wasn't easy. Goodness, that reminds me of the "God-shaped vacuum" concept that we often discussed on earth. You know how that one goes. Everybody is born having a God-shaped vacuum. People who don't want to acknowledge God try and fill the vacuum with everything but God — money, possessions, pleasure. In the end nothing satisfies, because nothing else fits that God-shaped vacuum. I guess you, my precious family, have a Jay-shaped vacuum that is difficult to fill. Let me give you a little tip. Only God can fill that vacuum, as well. Nobody else can, and nothing else will. In my newfound wisdom, I have learned that not only does God fill vacuums, He truly is the source of all wisdom and comfort. Draw your strength daily from Him. I'm getting so "preachy" here, you can just call me St. Jay! (That has a nice ring to it!) I'll just add one more thing. Remember those guardian angels that are watching over the three of you? They are still there. They never left you for a moment, not even on Christmas Eve and Christmas Day. I hope that you can draw some comfort from that.

On a lighter note, those angels will be following Mom and Holly around as they do their January bargain hunting. Please give them a break! They loathe ladies' boutiques. Too boring!

How did I celebrate Christmas? First and foremost, I celebrated it in the company of "the birthday boy" Himself, Jesus Christ. Now, that's special. On Christmas Eve, a multitude of people gathered around the throne in commemoration of a night in history that cannot be surpassed. I can't possibly describe the evening in a way that you can fully understand, but I am going to toss out "bits and fragments" which will hopefully give you a "feel" for what transpired.

Thousands, perhaps even millions of people, thronged around the shores of the crystal sea. I have never attempted to describe this lake to you in any great detail, because it defies description. Some of the people stood; others sat. The air was electric with anticipation and excitement. An enormous choir of angels had been singing carols all evening, carols that I've never heard before and that almost overwhelmed me with their poignant beauty. Soon, the people joined their voices to those of the angel choir in a glorious medley of praise and thanksgiving. The refrain of one of the songs went something like this: "Glory to the almighty God, the creator of heaven and earth, and glory to His son, the risen Lamb of God." In the midst of all this glorious worship and praise, a recreation of some of the events of that first Christmas night were taking place. The central figure of the Christmas story was, of course, still Jesus, but it was not the baby Jesus in a cradle that had our attention. It was Jesus as the "King of Kings" - He who sits at the right hand of God. He sat on the throne in all His kingly splendour. The shepherds that came to see the baby Jesus were there in full costume; they filed in and knelt before the throne. Then I saw several men, dressed in magnificent, kingly robes, approach the throne. "Ah, the wise men," I thought to myself. Suddenly it occurred to me that none of these people were actors. They were, in fact, the original cast — the shepherds from the hillside; the wise men from the orient who brought Him gifts of gold, frankincense and myrrh. The pageantry and the music went on for hours and finally culminated in groups of children carrying aloft a variety of enormous birthday cakes. They sang in perfect harmony, "Glorious birthday to you, glorious birthday to you, glorious birthday, dear Jesus, glorious birthday to you." Jesus cut up the cakes expertly with a golden sword, and the children distributed the pieces of cake to every person in the crowd. At the risk of sounding carnal, I have to admit that I had more than one piece. (But, who's counting?)

For awhile, people continued to fellowship in small groups.

Children ran around and played. I wondered what they were waiting around for. The festivities appeared to be over. I soon realized, however, that they were far from over.

A long queue formed rapidly along the shores of lake. I noticed that Jesus was sitting on the throne. He had removed His crown, and His hands were already reaching out towards the first people in the line-up. It seemed people were not prepared to go home until they had individually met with Jesus. Eagerly, I joined the queue. It moved along with surprising rapidity, considering that Jesus had a special word for everybody. Heaven's clock cannot be measured by earthly concepts of time.

The more I have become acquainted with this place and its people, the more mysterious it gets. I've been here for over four months now and have learned so much, and yet I feel like I have barely begun to discover its mysteries. It has been a wonderful four months of composing and playing beautiful music, of studying and learning, of meeting scores of wonderful people, and of leisurely pursuits that I never had time for on earth. I have had no sense of anything missing from my life, and yet have had the conviction from the beginning that my departure from earth had a very profound purpose, and that one day, very soon, that purpose would be revealed to me.

On this Christmas Eve, as I knelt before the throne of Jesus Christ, I felt an overwhelming sense of peace and anticipation. As Jesus placed his hand on my head, I heard him say very softly, "Child, there are many reasons why I have brought you here in what appears to be a premature manner. Some of those reasons will be worked out on earth for My honour and glory. Many young people were greatly affected by your departure from earth, and souls have been saved because of it. More souls will be reached in the future through the people you touched. The earthly harvest will one day astound you. However, some of the reasons will be worked out right here in heaven, and very soon. You see, my son, I needed a young, talented musician for a very special purpose, and I think you fit the bill perfectly. Very soon, my good friend John, will fill you in as to what's going to be happening." I looked to the left of Jesus, and saw a good-looking, blonde fellow. I knew this had to be John, Jesus' beloved disciple. John smiled at me warmly, and patted me on the shoulder. "We'll get together real soon, Jay," he said. "I think you're almost ready for the task we have in mind for you. By the way, have you been enjoying yourself?" he asked. "Oh, it's been heavenly," I exclaimed. We both laughed at my choice of words. "So," I continued, "what's the task that you have in mind?" "Wait and see," he said with a smile, "but I would suggest you keep those guitar strings in good working order." Wow! At the moment my head is spinning, and I obviously cannot share information I don't have yet, but my next letter should be an eye-opener!

Following my special time with Jesus and John, I dazedly walked around for awhile. However, soon my head began to clear, and I suddenly spied Oma on the other side of the lake in the midst of a group of noisy, laughing people. I wandered over towards them and had the pleasure of being introduced to some very interesting people that I hadn't met thus far. Maybe I couldn't be with you on Christmas Eve, but I sure wasn't bereft of family. Oma introduced me to a young woman she called "Celia". She looked very much like Oma — the same dark, curly hair and laughing, blue-grey eyes. I wracked my brain for a moment, and suddenly remembered the connection. You see, Mom, I did listen to your rambling stories of the past, even when it appeared I wasn't paying attention. Celia is the eleven year old daughter that Oma lost many, many years ago — long before you were born. I guess that would make her your half-sister, and my aunt. I don't know what kind of a relationship I'm supposed to have with an aunt, but this girl is fun. We immediately "clicked". She told me she was a gymnast, and as I get to know her better, I guess I'll find out what a gymnast actually does in heaven. I have this ridiculous picture of her doing cartwheels all up and down the golden streets of heaven. Oma also introduced me to her parents (my great grandparents) and several of her brothers and sisters. I vaguely remembered Uncle Reinhold from an old picture album at Aunt Dru's house. This is one place where Mom has just as many relatives as Dad! I know Mom has always been envious of Dad's large family.

Speaking of Dad's family, since it is Christmas, and a time for families, I made a special point of visiting with Grandpa earlier today — before the festivities even began. He was delighted to see me, and introduced me to a number of relatives on the Kehler side. I guess the one you'd be most interested in is your brother Abe, Dad. I have so many uncles below, but only two up here. I told Uncle Abe that he did not look like the rest of the Kehler boys, and he laughed and said he'd been told that all his life. He figured he was better looking than the other brothers, even when he was still on earth. He offered to take me out fishing one day. Apparently he knows where and when the fish are biting. And no, you can't just pick them out of the water with your bare hands. That wouldn't be any fun. I told Uncle Abe I'd love to go, but that I would have to wait until I find out what my new responsibilities were. He nodded wisely and said, "There'll be time, don't worry!" I got the distinct impression that he's involved in some very special work, too, but still has time to go fishing.

Writing letters is a very tedious job. I wonder why nobody has come up with the idea of erecting a telephone hot-line from heaven to earth. Hmm! Then we could talk for hours, just as we did when I used to call on Saturday nights from the camp that I was working at last summer. (And this time, you wouldn't have to pay the bill!) On the other hand, maybe that isn't such a good idea. It's good for you to hear from me; I'm not sure I really want to hear from you. No offense, but you earthlings carry a lot of excess baggage around. Stuff like sin and sorrow, worry and cares! I think it would be best if I just let God deal with those things in your life. He can do something about them, whereas I can't. So, okay, forget that idea. I will graciously continue to write, provided you appreciate the sacrifice I'm making! (Just kidding, guys!)

You are going into a New Year. It would appear that this past year has hardly been idyllic — Holly's eye problems, Dad's muscle disease, my departure from earth. This does not compute by earthly standards. However, try to look at it through "heavenly eyes." Holly has a special gift of sight that she doesn't need two good eyes for. She sees the needs of others, and has a great gift of encouragement. Dad's guardian angel is busily working on a formula for decreasing the constant pain; perhaps he'll have to allow the angel to carry him more. Mom seems to have begun a compassionate ministry to hurting people, and as for my departure — well — it's not as though you don't know where I am. I haven't disappeared without a trace. Wasn't it you, Mom and Dad, who always told me as long as you know where I am and what I'm doing, you could relax? So, relax! You know I'm safe. As a matter of fact, I'm more than safe. I'm redeemed. That shell that you buried wasn't me. I am alive! I've had victory over sin and death. Just think of heaven as Hawaii — except better! You've received enough exotic postcards to appreciate this:

> *Hi, Guys!*
> *Wonderful place. Having a marvellous time. Will come back when the boss returns. Wish you were here. Won't be long!*
>
> > *Until then,*
> > *Love, Jay*

Letters from Heaven

January 26, 1994

Dear Mom, Dad & Holly,

The above date won't have much significance for anybody else, but it is somewhat of an occasion for the Kehler family. Incidentally, I did remember that it is Oma's earthly birthday today, as well. I shared with her that our family had made a new occasion out of her birthday, one called "Children's Day." She wanted to know all about it, and seemed quite "tickled" that we would commemorate our Children's Day on her birthday. As I was telling Oma about all this, a number of other people gathered 'round, and wanted to know what kind of a holiday this was? What kind of a holiday, indeed? I had to tell them it was one that my parents invented due to pressure from their two children, who felt that it was only fair that if there be a Mother's Day, and a Father's Day, that there also be a Children's Day. Voila! January 26th.

As I reflect upon past Children's Days, I can't help but think that this one won't have been much different — other than the fact that I couldn't attend. Mom and Dad aren't that innovative! The three of you went out for dinner, right? Actually, I have a feeling there was four of you, because knowing Holly, she would insist on taking a friend. Or, knowing my family in general, there's probably another child or young adult currently living with you. Regardless, in the past couple of years the choice of restaurants was always a point of contention, with me wanting Chinese food, and Holly wanting a fast food place. Knowing you, Holly, you probably decided to go for Chinese food this year, just to spite me.

No doubt, Mom and Dad came up with their usual "just a little something" gift!? Hey, Mom and Dad, I'm not criticizing. I understand that you were still broke from Christmas. Anyway, the small (but meaningful) gift that you gave us was always appreciated. Right, Holly? (Say yes, child, you still have to live with them!) All in all, Children's Day is a nice concept, and considering that ninety-nine and nine-tenths of the world doesn't celebrate it, we were ahead of most kids. Anything that ties a family together is cool. Anything that ties a family together for all eternity is even better. As I've mentioned over and over, there is no unhappiness and sorrow here in heaven, but wow — you should hear the rejoicing when another family member and another loved one arrives here safely. I don't want you guys rushing to get here, but I'm so excited that all three of you will eventually show up. I am sorry for your sake that you had to celebrate Children's Day without me this year, but we'll make up for it "in the sweet bye and bye."

I thought by now I would have some exciting news to share with you regarding the conversation I had with Jesus and John on Christmas Eve. However, I haven't really heard much more. I know they haven't forgotten me, because every time I see them, they encourage me to keep practicing my guitar. As a matter of fact, the other day when I was talking to John, he asked me to review some of my earth music. Now, that's a strange request, don't you think? The music up here is so superior to anything that I played on earth, it's almost insulting to go back to that. I say "almost" because if Jesus or John request it, it's okay. There's a good reason. Being in God's will makes good sense on earth; it makes perfect sense here. And so, I'll wait — exercising my newfound heavenly patience. When I know what Jesus has in mind for me, I'll be more than happy to share it with you.

In the meantime, I have other interesting news. I took a fishing trip with Uncle Abe, the first of many, I hope. He took me to his favourite "fishing hole". Actually, the fishing hole was an enormous, picturesque lake on the far side of a low range of mountains. On one side lies my animal park; on the other side this beautiful lake. I wish I could use our heavenly language to describe the surroundings, or at the very least, have Mom's gift of description. All I can say, is, this place simply blew me away. We prop-drifted towards the sandy, white beach. The weather, as usual, was perfect. Golden and balmy. At this point I would have been quite content to slip back into childhood and lazily begin the sand castle routine, but Uncle Abe wouldn't let me. He's a very serious fisherman. I wasn't overly surprised to see a number of small, wooden boats anchored along the edge of the lake. After being here for awhile, you begin to take some of these little conveniences for granted. Uncle Abe led me confidently towards the one painted a glistening blue and white. Apparently it's his favorite one, and today, happily, it was available. Several very sophisticated fishing rods lay in the boat. I couldn't believe people would leave expensive equipment like that laying around. Upon mentioning my concern to Uncle Abe, he started to laugh. After a minute I began to laugh, too. Even after six months, I have to keep reminding myself that earthly values no longer apply. Nobody is going to steal the rods, and they're obviously not going to rust. I breathed in, deeply. The air seemed unusually fresh and pure this morning. The boat drifted lazily along the surface of the lake. Uncle Abe and I talked — some. According to him, the fish don't bite when you "natter" too much, so our conversation soon tapered off. The fish didn't exactly jump into the boat, but I did eventually land a couple of good- sized pickerel. Uncle Abe said they weren't quite like the pickerel on earth, but close enough, and even better tasting. When we came back to shore, we built a small fire. Uncle Abe scrounged around in the bushes nearby and found some large leaves. We wrapped the fish in the leaves and baked them in the fire. Mmmm! After a lazy snooze on the beach, we woke up to find the white sand around us clean and unblemished. Uncle Abe told me that there is a special agent in the air that absorbs and cleanses all impurities. The black marks from the fire had mysteriously disappeared. We swam and prop-drifted in the lake for a couple of hours and eventually prop-drifted back home, feeling satiated and refreshed. What a day! And so we go from peak to peak, exploring this vast and glorious kingdom.

Several months ago I mentioned that I was continuing my studies. I neglected to mention, however, the beautiful setting in which I attend these various classes. There's a group of buildings fairly near to the downtown core of heaven which we have lovingly dubbed "The Great Halls of Learning." It looks a little like an earthly university campus, but much larger than any I ever saw on earth. The buildings are situated on the crest of a steep hill and are made of rose, blue, green and white colored marble. There are stairs leading upward towards the great brass doors. Some people like to walk up the stairs, the earth way. Others prop-drift. As I mentioned earlier, we don't have night and darkness here, but there are graduations of light throughout the day. The Great Halls of Learning look particularly beautiful in the early part of the day, as the soft rose, blue and green meshes together in the dazzling morning light to form a rainbow effect. Mom's "writing" is going to take on new dimensions up here. Poetry screams out of every building, every tree, every flower, every blade of grass. Speaking of trees and flowers and grass, the grounds of the buildings are beautifully kept. Don't forget that nothing ever wilts or rots or dies. I've seen a few gardeners roaming around the grounds, and they seem to be very busy. Since they obviously don't have to fight weeds, I wonder how they keep themselves so occupied. They're probably into more creative gardening, such as cross-something-or-other. (You can sort of tell that my knowledge of gardening is still very limited. Horticulture is your thing, Dad, not mine).

I am getting off the track here. I was going to tell you about my studies. I am finding history particularly fascinating since I arrived here, so I've been taking a number of history courses. I've slipped into Jesus' theology classes whenever there's room. There's a distinct difference between the format of Jesus' classes and the other classes that I have been attending. In the other classes, there's a lot of discussion going on, perhaps even what could be termed as

Lilli Kehler

friendly arguments. In Jesus' classes there is an almost holy hush. Everybody hangs on to His every word, hardly daring to breathe. During the question and answer time, every ear strains to hear His answers. It has made me realize anew, that whether it be heaven or earth, He is the authority. The alpha and omega. The beginning and the end. I still haven't ventured near the business classes, but I'm starting to mellow. One of these days I may drop in. It would be interesting to learn how a huge kingdom like this is run so efficiently and painlessly. When I see the business classes, I am always reminded of Dad. He always seems to feel the need to organize something, somewhere. In recent years, his health problems have held him back. Just think, Dad, what you'll be able to accomplish up here with God's Royal Bank (?!) at your disposal and a body that isn't limited by pain and fatigue.

This letter must come to a close. However, since this is a Children's Day letter, I did want to add one or two things about children. Going out for dinner once a year to commemorate Children's Day is a nice thought, Mom and Dad. It made us feel very special. But the best thing you ever did for me was introduce me to Jesus Christ and His love. At the age of five, with your help, Dad, I accepted Jesus Christ into my heart and life. I am where I am today because of that decision. So many parents out there do everything for their children, except the most important thing of all — preparing them for eternity! Thanks, Mom and Dad, for giving your children the very best!

Your favourite son, Jay

Letters from Heaven

February 14, 1994
Dear Mom, Holly & Dad,

The letters are going out to you thick and fast. It seems like I just wrote, and here I am again. Happy Valentine's Day, all of you!

No doubt, Dad gave Mom a "sappy" Valentine's card, as usual. He's so hopelessly sentimental. And Mom just laps it up, year after year. In response to this tiny note of sarcasm, a small voice in my head pipes up, insistently: "Don't knock it, son. The love they share created a nice, stable environment for you to grow up in. Would you have preferred a war zone in your home?" I suppose not! Hey, Holly, do you ever wonder what they talk about when they go out for coffee by themselves? For hours and hours? After 30 years of marriage you'd think there wouldn't be anything worthwhile left to discuss. They probably talk incessantly about us. What a blessing we've been to them, and all that kind of parental hoopla!!

How's your love life, Holly? Is there anybody in your life that I wouldn't approve of? Just because I'm not there to keep an eye on you, doesn't mean you're not being watched. Miko is the name of your guardian angel, and he informs me that you're not an easy person to guard. Don't you ever rest? Give the poor guy a break, okay? He'd like you to settle in to one church, one youth group, one group of friends. Instead, you've got him running around in circles trying to keep up with you. Now, listen to your big brother, Holly. You need to spend time with the Lord, and you need to get enough rest. I know that I wasn't always the greatest example of that when I was on earth, but remember, I see more clearly now. So, listen and learn. Incidentally, occasionally Mom and Dad do make good sense, too, so heed their advice. In the meantime, Miko is hanging in there. He has become quite fond of you, in spite of your hyper schedule, and is committed to protecting you. He thinks his job will become even more demanding when you get your driver's license, so a little break now and then would be much appreciated. He sleeps when you do. And no, I'm not contradicting myself. We don't need to sleep in heaven, but when ambassadors from heaven are temporarily on earth, they begin to succumb to some of earth's restrictions. Goodness, how did I digress so far from Valentine's Day? Let me get back to the theme at hand.

On earth, Valentine's Day is a special one-day celebration of love. In heaven, love is celebrated without beginning or end. As best as I can describe it, an all pervasive love seems to emanate from the throne of God. It wraps itself around us like a warm, silken cocoon. When we are thus daily enveloped in God's love, it is not a hardship to love those around us, especially in light of the fact that people are so responsive and loving in return. Add to that the fact that all of earth's jealousies, prejudices, pain and greed have been washed away, and the result is an atmosphere of happy harmony.

Let me illustrate this on a practical level. I have become good

Letters from Heaven

friends with a fellow by the name of Jared Johnson. What has primarily drawn us together is our love for music. He plays the guitar and sings, and he does both extremely well. For a number of years, he was the lead singer in a secular rock band. Just a short time before he came to heaven, he became a Christian. His life began to move into a different direction. I think he would eventually have had a marvellous ministry to young people, but God took him before that became possible. Heaven has given me skills on the guitar that I never dreamed possible, and my voice has improved considerably, but I have to admit that Jared has me beat on both counts. He began with a natural gift and spent much time and money developing it. He's had years of guitar lessons from one of the world's finest teachers. Under normal earth circumstances, I think I could have been quite jealous of his talent. Here, it doesn't seem to matter. He enjoys my compositions; I enjoy the way he sings and plays them. He is also most willing and eager to share his knowledge with me, and so I've learned much from him in the short time I've known him. While I'm learning musical skills from him, I have been able to share insights about Christ and heaven that he didn't seem to know — probably because he hadn't been a Christian very long. He is just so excited about being in heaven and so relieved that he accepted Christ before it was too late. Although there is no sadness in heaven, there is very real concern, and Jared is concerned about the family he left on earth. To the best of our knowledge, none of them are Christians. I'm glad that I don't need to be concerned about my family. Just make sure you marry a fellow that's a Christian, Holly, and then we're all set. My point in all of this is that, because there is no jealousy and greed here, love can abound. When all of one's needs are met and satisfied day after day, love has free reign.

Now for the exciting news that we've all been waiting for. Talking about Jared reminded me, because he's going to be involved too. I finally had that meeting with John regarding my future in heaven. He had several other guys with him. The names wouldn't mean anything to you, but they were "big suit-and-tie organizer types" (without the suits, of course). Here's the scoop. Apparently there are more and more people entering heaven that have made last minute decisions. In by-gone years, people were more prone to die of diseases and physical hardships, and thus were able to prepare themselves somewhat for eternity. In recent years, because of earth's so called progressiveness, there are more and more fatalities due to accidents. Many of these people live for a few days, a few hours, sometimes only for a few minutes. During these short moments, many of them recognize that they are going to die, and they cry out to the Lord to forgive them and to save them. Having met Jesus personally, I can fully understand why He cannot say "No" to these people. He's so tender and compassionate, and as scripture says, "He is not willing that any should perish."⁵ So they come into heaven by the skin of their teeth, knowing almost nothing of spiritual things. Some of them have lived very evil lives on earth, others merely self-centered lives, but the fact remains, that it is only by the grace of God that they have become fit to enter heaven. They are grateful that God has saved them from the hell they deserved, but they are also confused and disoriented.

Letters from Heaven

As John was reviewing all this, I began to see where he was going. Amongst all these casualties, there are many teenagers, many young adults. They never served God in their earthly lives, knew nothing about Him — and cared even less. They rarely or never attended church and had never participated in any kind of Christian youth activities. Some came from countries and cultures that worshipped other gods. Yet, somehow, in the end they were all confronted by the living God, and accepted Him as their personal Savior and Lord. An orientation process is needed, and that's where yours truly comes in. John has asked me to participate and give some leadership in an orientation program that includes music and discipling.

We still have a lot of planning and organizing to do, but this is how I see this thing developing. Since Jared and I will both be involved, we've had a lot of fun bouncing ideas back and forth. John said that other young people are being asked to participate, and very shortly we will be having a meeting to consolidate everything. I'm psyched. As I was saying, this is how I see this thing developing. I have no idea of the kind of numbers we are talking about, but I'm sure we could fill an enormous stadium; probably a number of stadiums. As these young people filter in, our bands could be playing some contemporary Christian earth music to make the transition less confusing. Later on in the program, we could make the shift to heavenly music. The contrast would be an illuminating experience, believe me. I can visualize gifted speakers who will begin the discipling process in the lives of these new converts. I can visualize workshops where people can divide up into small groups; where they can ask questions and interact. We're obviously going to need a variety of musicians, workshop leaders, keynote speakers, and people who are gifted in administration. I think I'd like to be a workshop leader as well as being involved in the musical praise and worship. Fortunately, here in heaven we don't need to fuss about food. People can just pluck fruit off the trees if they have a desire to eat. On the other hand, in every group and social situation that I've ever been in, there's always somebody that seems to have a need to pluck the fruit, artfully arrange it on a plate and pass it around. Having been gifted hosts and hostesses on earth, they can't seem to stop.

I would also like to see a wilderness camp organized for some small groups. Wilderness camps aren't "my thing", but I know that some young people enjoy them tremendously, and would instantly feel at home in such a setting. Orientation programs could be varied to fit individual needs. I should add that like everything else here, the wilderness is beautiful. I haven't had an opportunity to see it myself, but have heard stories of great, dense jungles and challenging whitewater rafting from people that have been there. The possibilities are endless. I'll keep you informed as we move along, but I think this orientation process is going to be an exciting adventure.

On that note, I must leave you. I'll write again at Easter. Let Valentine's Day be a reminder for you that in heaven, love is eternal, and let the approaching Easter season be a reminder that in heaven, life is eternal. What greater hope could we have?

Love, forever, Jay

Letters from Heaven

April 3, 1994
Dear Dad, Holly & Mom,

"He is risen!" That's how the early Christians greeted each other. And then, people would respond by saying, "He is risen indeed!" Personally, I think that's a far more creative greeting than "Hi, how's it going?" This is Easter Sunday, and all day there has been rejoicing here in heaven. Shouts of "He is risen" and "He's alive" and "He is Lord" have been ringing all over heaven proper. We don't have church bells in heaven, obviously, because we don't have churches, but the voices raised in praise to the risen Saviour have a bell-like quality. Maybe sound carries more clearly in this atmosphere because it doesn't have umpteen layers of smog and pollution to penetrate.

How was your Easter? Trickles of information about my family come to me through your guardian angels. Holly's angel, Miko, is particularly informative. I think it's because he gets so exasperated. He needs a sounding board so he pulls me aside occasionally for a heart-to-heart chat about my hyper sister. I'm afraid I'm not very helpful. I just shrug my shoulders and tell him, "It's a stage". The last time I told him that, he snorted and mumbled something about moving on to an easier guardianship...an elderly lady, I think. However, so far he hasn't made a change. He's still with you, Holly. I think he feels you're an investment, and he's quite proud of the fact that he helped you to get your driver's license. Congratulations, kiddo! I guess now we have to send out additional guardian angels to protect the rest of the world!

The Easter celebration today has been truly amazing. We don't have seasons in heaven such as we knew on earth — summer, winter, spring and fall. However, that doesn't mean we don't have change. There was a fresh, spring-like quality to the air. I prop-drifted to the morning Easter celebration amidst the sound of birds singing and people shouting "Hosanna". I encountered Jared along the way and we prop-drifted together, returning the greetings of people as we soared along. What a glorious morning. When we arrived at the crystal sea, hundreds of thousands of people were already seated on the ground, awaiting the arrival of Jesus. A rainbow of rich, emerald hues arched over the empty, golden throne. Situated on its great, high platform, it could be seen for miles around. Its shadowy twin shimmered and wavered in the glassy surface of the sea several hundred feet below the platform.

Jesus' arrival was hailed by the pure, sweet tones of three trumpeters. Brass instruments have never been my favourites, but this was most appropriate. Christ walked in with an entourage of people following him. I recognized John immediately. He is so close to Christ and yet so humble. I have had much interaction with John because of our orientation program, and consider him a close, personal friend. I also recognized Peter and several other disciples. I have not had the pleasure of meeting Peter thus far, but I hope I will, soon. He's another Bible character that I respected and admired so much in my earthly tenure. Back to Christ. He was wearing a crown, which is quite unusual. Normally the only thing that distinguishes Him from the rest of us is that aura of radiance and light that continually surrounds Him. Studded with rubies, diamonds, pearls and emeralds, the crown blazed boldly in the morning light. His face shone with love and the usual aura of light encircled him like a gentle spotlight. People fell on their faces as He walked in. A choir of angels began to sing another one of those songs that only heaven knows, "Hosanna to the King of Kings." People took up the chant, and soon thousands of voices were raised in pulsing praise to the Saviour and Ruler of heaven and earth. Before sitting down upon the throne, Christ stretched out His hands to the people gathered around the lake, and as they once again saw His nail-scarred palms, the applause became tumultuous. Because of those nail-scarred hands, we will live forever. Jesus paid for our tickets to heaven, and we will be eternally grateful.

The celebrations went on all day. There were speeches and music and entertainment and food. It was a giant "Sonfest", and the guest of honour was the Son of God. Think about that when you attend "Sonfest" at the Abbotsford Airport this year, Holly. Hopefully, all that is said and done there is also to glorify the Son of God and uplift the hearts of people.

Time in heaven is a strange and wondrous thing. We keep very, very busy and yet life appears to be so relaxed. Everybody has an important job to do and yet everybody seems to have plenty of leisure time. There is such a wonderful balance of work and play and rest. "Rest?" you say. "Why would people in heaven need to rest?" As I mentioned in another letter, they don't. We seem to have a limitless supply of energy and don't need restorative sleep and rest. However, sometimes we desire it, and so we take it. I find every time I go down to my animal park, I take time to rest. Recently I revisited that area with a group of newcomers. They were delighted with it. Some of them went horseback riding, some of them golfed, some of them just chased around after the animals. Me? I found that same lazy, gray and white cat that reminds me of Jingles, put her on my chest and fell asleep. It must be some kind of earthly throwback, but I thoroughly enjoy my little snoozes. Maybe I'm still catching up from my university "all-nighters".

I have had another one of those marvellous fishing trips with Uncle Abe. This time another uncle joined us, Uncle Melvin. I vaguely remembered him, although since I grew up in another part of the country, I never got to know him very well. However, we both remembered one particular visit to his farm when I was just a little kid — a little "city kid", I might add. Uncle Melvin's dirt bike fascinated me. It looked so easy when he or my cousin, Joe, drove it. I begged and pleaded to be allowed to try it out. Poor Uncle Melvin certainly learned to run in circles that day. I had no problem driving the bike; it's just that I forgot how to stop it!

We rowed out into the middle of the lake, where according to Uncle Abe, fish are the most plentiful. There was a bit of a breeze that day, just enough to make the rowing a little easier. Uncle Abe and I both caught a couple of fish each, but Uncle Melvin caught nothing. I think he's too restless; he scares the fish away. He's great for a laugh, though. He chuckled when I told him that I attended a Mennonite Brethren church on earth. He wondered what my "hard-core Baptist" parents thought of that. I had forgotten that he was a former pastor. I told him jokingly that I had to overlook some of the inconsistencies in the M.B. church in order to get a more enlightened music program. He laughed at that. When I asked him what his responsibilities were here in heaven, he mentioned something about a large workshop, but he didn't go into specifics. Just asked me to drop by his place one day and see. His parting shot before he left us was, "By the way, Jay, make sure you do some research about the M.B.'s before we meet again; this discussion isn't finished yet." I'll bet it isn't! And, I think I'm in trouble!

I had a game of tennis the other day with Kirsten, Danny and another friend by the name of Danielle. I met Danielle through Kirsten. Apparently the two girls met the first day they came to heaven. Both were involved in auto accidents on the same day on earth, although in different parts of the country. Danielle and I skunked Danny and Kirsten, so they, of course, are anxious for a rematch. I've been so involved in helping to get this orientation program off the ground, that tennis will have to be put on a back burner for awhile.

Regarding the orientation program, we are off and running. The first orientation took place a couple of weeks ago. Prior to that, we had a large planning conference with all interested parties. John gave a brief introductory speech as to the purpose and goals of this operation, and then we formed into smaller groups to brainstorm and to ascertain everybody's responsibilities. It was my first experience with a "committee" here in heaven and it wasn't that much different from the committee meetings I used to attend on earth. Somehow I expected everybody to instantaneously agree on everything, but that didn't happen. Different people had different opinions on how things should be done. Ultimately, just like on earth, we compromised. The big difference here is that when we finally concluded our plans, everybody was totally satisfied. We had reached a consensus that everybody was happy with. The Bible calls it "being in one accord". If I recall correctly, "being in one accord" on earth was a very elusive phenomenon. John had appointed me as one of the orientation concert leaders. In other words, I have been put in charge of one particular concert group that reaches out to a segment of the "new immigrants" coming in. During our small group sessions, I was also chosen to be leader of a workshop.

That first concert was a complete high! Our leadership group, which consists of Jared, myself and eight other young people, had written and rehearsed some earth music. We had also discovered a natural amphitheatre on the outskirts of heaven proper which lent itself beautifully to what we were trying to accomplish. Kids from the ages of about 13 to 25 were directed to our huge outdoor amphitheatre, and as they filed in, I saw some of them exchange relieved looks with each other. We had erected a giant stage on a low hill, and I could tell that the familiar sight of drums, guitars and

Letters from Heaven

keyboards on the stage were of comfort to them. The only thing missing was miles of electric cord. I had written a special orientation song for the occasion and as soon as everybody sat down, our group began to sing and play. Just a little aside here... we didn't need to set up any chairs for the occasion. The ground has a peculiar sponginess that makes it very comfortable for sitting on. Back to the orientation song, since this is an earth piece, I can share the words with you. The melody is upbeat and fast, and in no time, we had everybody clapping and moving with the rhythm of the music.

Lilli Kehler

It's a Different World, but the Music Goes On!

Death and darkness have surrendered their claim,
We awaken to a bright new dawn,
Forever changed, nothing the same,
It's a different world...
But the music goes on!

Chorus:

It's a different world,
But the music goes on,
All creatures, large and small,
Raise their voices
In worship and praise,
To the One Who created it all.

Evil is defeated in Jesus' sweet name,
Old things have passed; they are gone,
Troubles are over; no sorrow, no pain,
It's a different world...
But the music goes on!

(Repeat chorus)

A glorious new world, unspoiled, unstained,
A kingdom to depend upon,
Unspeakable joy, everlasting gain,
It's a different world...
But the music goes on!

(Repeat chorus)

Letters from Heaven

Yes, the music went on...and on...and on! Much later in the program, John introduced himself to the kids, and briefly explained the purpose of this orientation. Each of the kids had met Jesus as they entered into heaven, but now John ushered Him in to address them as a whole. The shallow valley that the kids were sitting in was so quiet you could hear a pin drop. Christ's love reached out to each one of them as individuals. It was as palpable as a touch. He had died on the cross for each one of these kids. Don't forget that most of them were last-minute converts. They felt very undeserving of heaven, but Christ's words and unconditional love soothed and comforted and challenged them. By the time the workshops began, the kids were beginning to feel very much at home. My workshop had a very basic theme: "God's Grace in Heaven and on Earth." Well, I could go on and on, but enough said for today. I'll share more about this in my next letter.

Dad, your birthday is coming up shortly. Happy Birthday, Mr. Half-Century. Do something nice for yourself and consider it a present from me. I love you, even if you are old and gray! I've been telling everybody up here about your therapeutic foot-rubs and they'll be lining up for a demonstration as soon as you get here. Of course, I get the first one — not because I have sore feet, but to enable you to show off your expertise in this area! Your guardian angel is watching over you very carefully. His name is "Healer" and he's still working on a formula to restore your health. In the meantime, he's there for your encouragement and protection. Just a word of admonition on his behalf, though. You know you shouldn't cut both the front and back lawn in one morning - especially on a hot day. Healer can't do anything for you if you're going to be unreasonable. So, please pace yourself a little more carefully from now on. I know how impatient you are, Dad, but try and remember that a slightly overgrown lawn does not constitute the unpardonable sin.

I have to close, but I love all three of you. I miss you. I know you miss me, too, but in Christ we have hope. The hope that you have, has already been fulfilled in my life. Hang in there, guys, and hang on to the One who makes it all possible. He is risen! And so am I!

Love, Jay

Letters from Heaven

May 8, 1994

Dear Mom, Dad & Holly,

Mom's name is first today, because, well, Happy Mother's Day, Mom! I don't think I was ever known for my great sensitivity on earth, but I do better now, and I recognize that this must have been an especially difficult day for you. To wish you a "happy" day would probably be stretching it, but I hope it was, at least, a bearable day for you. Moms want to spend Mother's Day with all their children and you're missing a full fifty percent of your lot. I wish that somehow I could be of special comfort to you on this occasion, but I'm going to have to leave that to our Saviour. Holly, of course, is with you "in the flesh". I know you'll enjoy her. As Miko, her guardian angel puts it, "She's a constant source of entertainment." As far as I'm concerned, I can't be there in the flesh, but my love for you is very strong and real, and it goes out to you over the miles. (This is beginning to sound like one of those sentimental Mother's Day cards that Moms always hope to get from their children, but hardly ever do!) As a matter of fact, I would have to say that my love is stronger and more perfect than it ever was on earth, so I pray that you would sense it in a special way today. I hope Dad also remembered to buy you a watch as a gift on my behalf. I put a bug in his ear about it, and knowing Dad's taste, he purchased a nice one for you. I can't resist the temptation to add that his taste in gifts has always exceeded his taste in clothes! I also can't resist the temptation to remind Mom what a watch is for - like, to get places on time! Before I get myself into big trouble, I'll move along to other subjects.

It is a particularly lovely day in heaven today. God has a special love for mothers, both on earth and in heaven. I prop-drifted over to the other side of the crystal lake today and went to see Oma. Celia was already there, as well as a few other relatives. We had a great time. I had not seen Celia for a while and enjoyed visiting with her. As I mentioned in an earlier letter, she's extremely athletic. She teaches gymnastics to people of all ages. One of these days I'm going to pop into her studio and observe. I'll do this very unobtrusively, because if Celia knows I'm there, she'll promptly have me on the floor turning myself inside out. If I'm going to exercise, I'll stick to tennis, thank you! The longer I'm in heaven, the more amazed I am at how people occupy themselves. With the help of Jesus, John and a number of other heavenly administrators, people seem to find their perfect niches. Just like I have!

Oma is doing fine. She was hustling and bustling about today, making sure everybody had enough to eat. I found myself dredging up an assortment of bad jokes just so I could hear her laugh. After we had lunch, several of us (including Oma) got out our guitars and began to jamm. It wasn't long before everybody there got down to the serious business of clapping their hands and stamping their feet. I watched Celia out of the corner of my eye and she was more than stamping her feet. She was dangerously close to dancing all over the place. I guess we have to forgive her. She loftily advised me that gymnastic instructors get special dispensation in heaven for exercising creative rhythm; it's part of their physical fitness training. Huh!

Later on in the day, Celia and I picked up some other friends and we all prop-drifted down to the animal park. There's so much to do down there, and as I mentioned earlier, the scenery is fabulous. Celia, of course, had to try out the mountain climbing, although the mountain there is really only a glorified hill. (Don't tell her I said that. She thinks she's in the big league!) A couple of other friends went horseback riding - after they finally managed to catch their horses. Jared and I lazily swam and prop-drifted around in the nearby lake. Eventually, we sat down at the bottom of the lake and sifted through the beautiful, jewel-like stones. We could hear strains of music floating around us, very different from the tones we or the angels produce up in heaven proper. Jared and I eventually caught the drift of the melody and began to sing along. At the risk of sounding corny, it was almost as though the stones and the waves around us were harmonizing in a song of praise to Jesus Christ. Forgive me, guys, but this is heaven. I can't be expected to sound totally lucid. It was quite an experience.

In the evening we built a camp fire on the beach and roasted some food we found in a nearby vegetable garden. One food item tasted similar to a roast potato and the other had a definite sweet taste. They were mouth-watering. After that we sat around and talked and sang for awhile. Just as we were thinking about returning home, we saw Somebody walking towards us across the lake. Jesus

Lilli Kehler

is so easy to spot, because as I mentioned earlier, He is always bathed in diamond-white light. He sat down with us, and we quickly became aware that the fellowship we thought was so splendid a few minutes ago was just a poor shadow of what we were now experiencing. I have discovered that every time we are in the physical presence of Christ, we feel a sense of oneness and completeness that is quite extraordinary. His unconditional love envelops us and frees us. I realize in awe, again and again, that without Christ, even heaven with all of its wonders and beauty could never be satisfying and complete. At the centre of the universe is Christ. At the centre of heaven is Christ. When the old heaven and the old earth pass away, as someday they will, Christ will still be at the centre of the new heaven and the new earth. However, now I'm waxing heavily theological and I don't want to overtax your finite minds. (Does my superiority ever get to you? Hopefully not, as I can't seem to help what I have become!)

Speaking about satisfying, I continue to find my role in the "heaven orientation program" immensely satisfying. I'm doing what I like to do best and in the process, am helping young people to adapt and integrate. I had to deal with a rather interesting case in one of my workshops. As I went through the steps of "God's Grace in Heaven and on Earth", I noticed a young man leaving the session. After the workshop was over, I followed him. I could see he was genuinely upset and as we began to speak, his story unfolded. He had been severely injured in a motorcycle accident, but had lived for three days before he finally entered into eternity. During those three days, in one of his lucid, conscious moments he realized that he was probably not going to "make it." His mother had taken him to Sunday School when he was a child, and he remembered having accepted Jesus Christ as his personal Saviour at a very young age. While in his early teens, his mother died. His father, in trying to deal with his own grief and pain, completely ignored the young teen and my friend, in his loneliness, anger and frustration began a life that eventually blossomed into full scale rebellion. In recent years he had become hardened to the point where gang rape was a lark and murder a deed of honour. As he lay dying, his life, with all of its hideous implications, flashed before him. But, mercifully, he also remembered the commitment he had made to Jesus Christ as a very young lad. He remembered enough from his Sunday School lessons to realize that God is just and merciful to forgive those who ask for forgiveness. "I'm sorry, dear Jesus," he wept. "I don't know what happened to me, I don't know what went wrong, but whether I live or die, I want your forgiveness for all the terrible things I did. Please forgive me and make me clean and whole again." To make a long story short, he died the next day and entered into heaven, as we all do, by God's grace. It certainly wasn't because of his good deeds. So here he was, another sinner saved by grace. He had already been graciously welcomed by Jesus Christ, had felt His overwhelming, unconditional love, but now he wanted to see his mother, and this was of grave concern to him. He was so ashamed and so afraid. How could he ever face her? Well, I didn't know his mother personally, but I do know how the saints, in general, conduct themselves up here and I knew he had nothing to worry about. However, I couldn't seem to convince him. Right about that time, I was glad I had a hierarchy to go to. I took him and the problem to my friend John. John has had two thousand years of experience in dealing with issues such as this; let him handle it.

He handled it. The other day I saw my young friend prop-drifting arm in arm with a sweet looking, blonde woman. They were obviously on their way to the crystal lake to see Jesus together, and they both looked so contented and happy. Heaven's peace! How can I adequately describe it to you earthlings? "The peace of God which passes all understanding" is finally understood![6]

Holly, I am quite cognizant of the fact that the month of May has other occasions besides Mother's Day. So, little "geek", Happy 18th Birthday *and* Happy High School Graduation! Wow, occasion upon occasion. How will you survive this month? Poor old Miko will be run ragged again, I'm sure.

I have been thinking and thinking about some great words of wisdom that I can offer you to cover both of these auspicious occasions. Short and sweet, here they are: **Be God's woman!** You are now a high school graduate and a young adult. Take responsibility for your own actions. Don't waste time on things that don't matter. Care for those that are weaker. Love the unloveable. Use the gifts and talents that God has given you. "In everything give thanks."[7] And last but not least, don't break guys' hearts! Treat the guys with the kind of courtesy and integrity that you expect from them. If you do all this, God will be honoured, Mom and Dad will be proud of you, I will expound your virtues to poor, weary Miko, and finally, you may eventually even wind up winning the Trinity Western

Letters from Heaven

Citizenship award (like I did, in case you've forgotten!). In re-reading the above paragraph, I realize that I've come a long way from the older brother that used to pull your hair and make fun of you. Ah well, we all have to grow up! And you, dear little sister, are doing a great job of it. (I just don't believe everything Miko tells me!)

Perhaps this is an appropriate time to share with you a discovery I made recently in "The Great Halls of Learning." I was on my way to a business class (yes, my curiosity got the better of me and I finally relented), when at the end of one great hall, I saw an enormous arrow pointing to the left. The sign beside the arrow said "Room 10, Book of Life." Since I still wasn't too sure about that business course, I was easily enough distracted. I found Room 10 and walked in. It was an enormous room, beautifully decorated. The ceiling had doves and cherubs painted across it. The walls were translucent pearl. Once again, I noticed that rosy sheen. Unlike most of the floors in heaven, this room was thickly carpeted in a soft shade of rose. Around the edge of the carpet was a marked off area in creamy-white. I'm describing this all for Mom's benefit. I know what she's like about decor, and it is Mother's Day, after all. In the centre of the room stood a huge, golden stand, and strategically placed upon this stand in a semi-upright position was an enormous gold and white book with its pages open. Something suddenly clicked inside my brain, and I was awe-struck by my discovery. This was the Book of Life, the Lamb's Book of Life - which had written in it all the names of those whose lives have been redeemed by the blood of the Lamb. In short, those who have inherited eternal

63

life. I pushed a small button on the stand, and the pages began to turn, slowly. The writing was large enough for Mom and Dad to read without their reading glasses! I kept flipping the pages. Some of the names had check marks beside them, and it occurred to me that these must be the people that were already here. As I continued to turn the pages, I began to recognize a few of the names. Several of the names that I recognized surprised me; I hadn't realized these people were Christians. I finally came to the K's, and there we all were. KEHLER, ERV. KEHLER, HOLLY. KEHLER, JAY (with a check mark beside it, confirming my "glorified status"). KEHLER, LILLI and KEHLER, BABY (referring, of course, to the little one that predeceased all of us). My throat felt tight and strange; this is probably as close to tears as I'll get in heaven. I read the names again and again, and the joy I felt was indescribable. Not that I had ever doubted that you would all join me one day, but to see it - right there in bold, flowing print - it was a moment of pure ecstasy!

I must close, once again. However, along with the ecstasy I felt in seeing your names in the "Lamb's Book of Life", I also have to share my concern. Every day there are newcomers to this place - children, young people, older folks. We see them arrive empty-handed, without luggage, without any personal possessions. When you see it from our perspective, the message is so clear and simple: "Only what's done for Christ will last". If everything else gets left behind, why are you spending so much time and money on it? Shouldn't you be spending the time and money on getting the message of salvation out to those whose names aren't written in the Book of Life? Are you getting the Word out to your friends and neighbours? What about to my friends? I want to see them all again some day. Don't grow weary, guys. This is just too important!

Lest it seem like I have totally ignored you in this letter, Dad, let me remind you that your day will come. Next month is Father's Day, and I am already thinking about what I can do for you in lieu of a foot massage and the usual gift of socks.

Love you all, Jay

Lilli Kehler

June 19, 1994

Hi Dad (and the rest of the family)!

I suppose I have to address the issue of "Father's Day" in much the same vein as "Mother's Day." I'm sorry I couldn't be there, Dad (sorry for your sake, not mine), but I do hope that the day had some light and joy in it. Certainly your daughter, Holly, can be all "sweetness and light" when she chooses to be, so I trust she used her considerable charm and skills to brighten your day. Incidentally, my dear, little sister, just because you're the only one currently mentioned in Mom and Dad's will, does not mean you're their only child. All it means is that I, their older child, have no need of an earthly inheritance. I am enjoying my role of joint-heir with Christ and it doesn't take a genius (or a business major) to figure out that my Father in heaven has considerably more wealth than my father on earth. I mention this not to make you jealous, Holly, but to firmly establish that just because I'm not in the will, does not mean I'm not in the family. I was born first. I was born again first. And, I was reborn first.

Back to you, Dad. I thought and thought about what I could give you for a Father's Day present. I wanted it to be something very special this year, something that would lift your spirit. I know you've got plenty of socks, and no doubt you've added my ties to

66

your collection. (Aren't my ties great? The girls I dated had exceptionally good taste!) I decided against a gift certificate to The Muffin Break. Traditional, old folks like you need to break out of your routine, and you've been patronizing that coffee shop long enough. I almost had Healer talked into a foot massage for you, but at the last minute he balked and said he didn't "do" feet. So, where does that leave me? Upon mulling it over at great length, I came to the conclusion that I can give you five very special **"thank you's."**

1.   First and foremost, Dad, **thank you** for leading me to the Lord at the age of five. You made me understand that I needed to invite Jesus Christ into my heart and life in order to get to heaven. I can now attest to the fact that because of that momentous decision, I am here! What were Jesus' exact words? "Except ye be converted, and become as little children, ye shall not enter into the kingdom of heaven."[8]

2.   Secondly, **thank you**, Dad, for role modelling the Christian life so effectively. Through thick and through thin, you have always tried to be God's servant - a man of faith, integrity and prayer. Since Mom has stuck with you for thirty years, I presume you must be a tolerably good husband, and you were certainly a patient father to Holly and me. Of course, Holly required more patience than I ever did, nevertheless, you did alright with both of us. Your bad jokes were only a minor irritant, and you dressed better as I got older.

3.   **Thank you**, Dad, for paying for all those years of music
        lessons. Organ, piano, drums, guitar. I'll bet you thought it
        would never end. Music was such an important part of my
        life growing up, and continues to be such a joy here in
        heaven. Truly, "the music goes on!"

4.   **Thank you**, Dad, for taking "moi" along on all those out-
        of-town business trips. You would pull me out of school for
        a week at a time, ply me with junk food and comic books
        while you made your sales calls, and then take me golfing
        or to the movies in the evenings. What a dream-come-true
        for a kid. I was the envy of all my classmates.

5.   And, last but not least, **thank you** for allowing me to make
        my own choices as I grew up. I realize they weren't always
        wise choices, but you let me go and covered me with prayer.
        I always knew I was bathed in prayer, and it gave me the
        courage to pick myself up when I fell, dust myself off, and
        begin again. That's called learning by experience, I guess.
        I have now grown beyond your wildest imaginings, but I
        am still your son, Dad. That will never change. I am still
        your son.

P. S.   Almost forgot. Thanks for teaching me to ride a bike, drive
        the car, cut the lawn (was that really necessary?), and play a
        decent game of golf. I never did beat you on earth, but you
        ought to see me now! Be prepared for some real competition
        when you get here.

Letters from Heaven

Well, there it is. I hope you enjoyed your present, and I love you, Dad.

Life for me continues to jog along smoothly. In one sense, heaven is an extension of earth in that I worship, I work, I play and I rest. In another sense, heaven is radically different, because we have shed all the shackles that bind and inhibit us on earth.

For example, I worshipped regularly on earth. Every Sunday, as a matter of fact, and often in between. However, much of the time my worship was fuzzy and lacked conviction. Perfect communion with God came so rarely because sin, sorrow and style got in the way. Here, sin has no hold on us, sorrow has been washed away, and style is not an issue. God's acceptance of worship is not based on style; it is based on the condition of the heart. Bended knees, raised hands, faces to the ground, lively enthusiasm and quiet praise - it's all the same to Him. The music here, for lack of a better expression, is "heavenly contemporary". God gives us a new song every day.

Continuing with my comparison, I worked hard on earth (sometimes), but didn't always find my jobs creative or fulfilling. Sometimes people became critical of my efforts, which dampened my spirit; other times I was plain old frustrated by the job itself. I had jobs that were so boring that I was just putting in time in order to earn the money. That doesn't happen in heaven. Since money is not an issue here, work is based solely on ability and availability. I find my work with the orientation team so rewarding, and even when

Lilli Kehler

I worked for the fellow who built my piano, it was a joyful, challenging experience. I obviously had no talent or expertise in this area, but it was my piano he was creating and it was fun to work alongside of him and learn how this beautiful instrument "works", inside and out.

The difference in play? Yes, I played tennis on earth, I golfed, I hiked and I "jammed" with my friends. Nothing has changed, and yet everything has changed. I am so physically fit, and my energy level is amazing. (That's not to say I never lose!) I guess "playing" becomes considerably more fun, too, when one never gets tennis elbow, sore muscles, or calloused fingers. I haven't missed the sore losers, either. While I'm on the topic, Dad, there are some great hockey and football teams up here, and we don't have to purchase Season's tickets. I've been to a few of the games and thoroughly enjoyed them, but I can hardly wait 'til you get here so we can, once again, cheer for opposite teams. It's more fun that way! Byetheway, I had to give up the hot dogs, but the popcorn more than makes up for it.

With regard to rest, I can vividly remember "crashing out" on my friends' beds in the dorms at Trinity because I was always so tired. All those busy days and late nights! Rest was certainly necessary, but it always seemed like such a waste of precious time. Now and then I also rest in heaven, knowing, of course, that I have all the time I'll ever need to complete my tasks. I rest, not because I'm exhausted, but as a pause, or a comma, to the many activities I am involved in. Reading a book on the swing on my verandah;

70

snoozing with the Jingles clone down at the animal park; softly strumming my guitar as I mentally compose a new song; meditating in quiet solitude beside a country stream; sitting companionably at the feet of Jesus as I listen to stories I've never heard before. This is heaven's sweet rest, and it nourishes, refreshes and revitalizes the spirit.

I'm almost done, folks, but I want to share yet another rather stunning experience with you. Several of my friends and I have been wanting to return to that beautiful valley and farm area that we discovered several months ago. One day last week we decided that this was the day. There were six of us, four guys and two girls.

We set out early and followed that same quaint little cobblestone road. After awhile, we switched into our prop-drifting gear and with amazing speed, headed towards the tip of the mountain. Nobody wanted to climb that day; we just wanted to explore. Once again, we stood at the top and gazed with admiration and awe at the lush valley below. As we made our swift descent, the sensations I felt were a little like those I used to experience at the Imax Theatre in Vancouver. A part of me was dizzyly preoccupied with keeping my balance, while another part of me was mesmerized by the beauty of the scene below. Eventually we reached the river. A number of large, log rafts were plying up and down the river. Gazing a little anxiously at the writhing, foaming waters, I wondered how safe the rafts were. There was general relieved laughter as Karen quipped, "Come on, guys. Don't look so worried. What's the worst than can happen?" What, indeed? A cool dip in the river? A benign bump on the head? An exhilarating walk on the water? We settled noisily onto one of the smaller rafts, and waited for our friendly captain to begin the guided tour. He was great - gregarious and informative. He told us a little about the people living along the banks, about their farming skills and wonderful orchards. He pointed out spectacular spots of interest along the way and plied us with home grown fruit juices. All in all, it was a very satisfying tour. Soon we had left the gracious estates far behind us and followed the river into wild, untamed countryside. At this point, we bid our new friend adieu and got off the raft. We were all in a very adventurous mood. Having begun this journey, we were determined to see it to some kind of grand conclusion.

We prop-drifted swiftly above the long meadow grasses. After we had covered a considerable distance, the wild, unkempt countryside gave way to gently rolling, manicured hills. From our vantage point, we saw the river fork off into smaller streams, which eventually fed into a number of small, sparkling lakes randomly tucked into the shallow valleys. They looked for all the world like tiny, blue patches on an intricate patchwork quilt. We drifted closer, and saw little towns and villages sprawled beside the lakes. We settled on one particularly picturesque village, and came to a halt. We looked in open mouthed wonder around us. The houses were small and quaint, of a design fashionable hundreds of years ago. But, there was no mistaking this for a "heavenly slum." The homes were sturdy and well built, and the gardens were beautifully tended. I saw flowers and shrubs that I haven't seen anywhere else in heaven. I felt like I had just wandered into a "Dickens Christmas card" and was, once again, astounded at God's versatility. The people living here would obviously view my spacious city home with great distaste. Their "mansions" were these snug, comfortable cottages beside the lake, where their men fished and their women wove the beautiful, white, linen-like cloth of the outfits we were wearing. We chatted to some of the villagers. They didn't seem surprised by our presence. We got the impression that they see lots of "tourists" and take them in their stride. One lady invited us into her small, but charming cottage for "tea and biscuits" and a chat. All in all, we had found our "conclusion", but along with it, came the awesome realization, once again, that we had not even begun to explore the wideness of God's mercy - geographically, culturally, or spiritually. There is still so much to come.

We eventually returned home, having been greatly enriched by our explorations. And so we go, as I've stated before, from peak to peak.

I must go. Other duties and pleasures call me. My next letter will come in August, for Mom's birthday, and for the first anniversary of my entry into heaven. How the year has flown - in spite of its sorrows for you - because of its joys for me! Doesn't it prove conclusively how quickly we'll be together again?

I'll sign off with Dad's ridiculous pet name for me...

Love, The Hoser

Lilli Kehler

August 2 & 7, 1994

Dear Mom, Dad & Holly,

Happy Birthday, Mom! Now that you have hit the mid-century mark as well, how do you feel? The neat thing about you and Dad being only four months apart is that you will both be drawing old age pension cheques at about the same time. On the other hand, the way things are going down there, there probably won't be any government pension money left by the time you both reach sixty-five, so you better start saving. On the other-other hand, perhaps there won't be any world left (as you know it) by the time you're sixty-five and then you'll have saved all that money for nothing. How about just trusting the Lord? Anyway, Mom, I hope reaching age fifty wasn't too traumatic for you, and as with every other occasion this past year, I'm sure you had mixed feelings. Perhaps we'll be together for your sixtieth, but in the meantime, I love you lots - in spite of (or perhaps because of) the fact that you're so short! (We can but hope that you'll be taller in heaven).

I don't think I have ever mentioned your guardian angel's name, Mom. Her name is Melody, and she has assured me that someday you will have a song in your heart again. It's been a tough year for you, but the joy will come back. Melody also assures me that she is watching over you, faithfully. She did question me about

74

your weird, nocturnal habits. I laughed and told her you had always been a night spook and that when I was on earth, I was the same way. Melody yawned and said that by and large she could handle that, provided she could catch a little nap in the daytime once in awhile. So, my dear, insomniac Mom, try and get some sleep before both you and Melody collapse. She'll become negligent in her duties if she doesn't get enough rest. All kidding aside, Mom, Melody is tough and strong and she'll stick with you.

I have also remembered, of course, that the month of August has another occasion besides Mom's birthday. August 7th is the first anniversary of my entry into heaven. For me, August 7th will always commemorate the excitement and joy I felt as I entered into the presence of my Saviour. However, I'm not insensitive as to what it commemorates for you — my departure from your world. Thus, I know that this has been an especially difficult week for you. Take heart, my family. All three guardian angels are in place and they have arranged for you all to be with good, caring friends during this time. I hope my letter will also help, reminding you once again that although you cannot see me and be with me, I'm more alive than you are. Above all, I know that Jesus Christ will be there to comfort you and surround you with His healing love. Don't forget that "the steadfast love of the Lord never ceases; His mercies never come to an end; they are new every morning; great is His faithfulness."[9] What more can I say, guys?

I have good news and bad news. The good news is, this is going to be an exceptionally long letter. The bad news is, this is going to be my last letter to you. My letters have, hopefully, helped you through your first long year of grief and pain, and now it is time to move on to other things - both for you, and for me. My life here is so full and so rich and I need to have the freedom to get on with it. Your lives need to move forward too; you must not be continually preoccupied with me. It is absurd to think we will ever forget each other, but the simple fact is, we need to give each other room to grow and expand. My friend, John, is continually heaping new and larger responsibilities upon me. As for you, I know that God has much for you to do, and you need to begin to do it. Dad, you have always been a "people person", and in spite of your health problems, your people ministry will gain exciting, new dimensions in the coming days. Mom, carry on writing. Contrary to how it may have appeared, Holly and I really did appreciate your attempts to expand our vocabularies. Continue to use your gift of "words" to minister to people. Holly, you need to turn Trinity Western University upside down, since I am no longer there to do it. God will surely send some hurting young people your way, and with your listening heart, I know you can make a difference.

Speaking of university, Holly, Miko proudly informed me that you just won the Minas Basin Scholarship award, the one that Dad's company grants each year. You little twerp! I applied for that scholarship four times and never got it. What makes you so special? The way Miko is swaggering around here, you'd think he was entirely responsible. Oh well, heaven does teach one to be gracious, so congratulations, little sis. I'm past all those infantile feelings of envy, jealousy and pride, so the fact that you received the scholarship

Letters from Heaven

and I didn't, doesn't disturb me at all. It's just that I really don't understand their rationale. I mean, if you compare our grades...! Seriously, kiddo, you deserve it and I'm happy for you. Enjoy your first year at Trinity, and remember the advice I gave you for your graduation. **Be God's woman**. (But I still don't understand why I never got that scholarship!)

Since this is going to be my last letter to you, I'm going to have to tie up a number of loose ends. Our orientation program is going great guns. Our numbers have increased a bit over the summer. I guess people travel more; swim more. About a month ago, we had a special praise and worship celebration at Crystal Lake. I wasn't playing in any of the worship bands that day, so I had the luxury of observing people around me. My interest was caught by a young guy, about my age. He had squeezed in as closely to the throne as possible, and was dancing up a storm, keeping perfect time to the music. Jesus was watching him with the same rapt attention I was. This guy's enthusiasm and excitement was contagious. After watching him for awhile, I sauntered over to him and complimented him on his graceful, easy style of motion. "I don't do so well with my feet," I told him, "but I can relate to your freedom of expression. I get that way when I've got a guitar in my arms, or if I'm sitting behind a set of drums." After chatting for a bit, he informed me that his name was Rick, and that he had just recently arrived. In swapping stories, I learned that he had "passed from death unto life" at a church camp in rural Manitoba. It seems that he jumped into the lake to rescue a drowning child — forgetting that he couldn't swim. He saved the child, but he, himself, drowned. He reminisced about his week at the camp. Since I, too, had been at a church camp when I left the earthly life, we found we had much in common. He told me that the praise and worship times at the camp had been awesome, but in retrospect, only a shadow of what he was experiencing here. "Worship and praise takes on a new dimension, doesn't it," he said, "when you're in the physical presence of Christ?" No doubt about that! "Furthermore," he said, "I can't believe this music. My feet just seem to develop little minds of their own." From my superior vantage point, I grandly informed him that "he hadn't seen nothin', yet!" He's a cool guy. I'm sure his family misses him terribly, but he's so thrilled to be here. We briefly discussed the ten year old boy whose life he saved, and came to the conclusion that God has a unique purpose for that kid's life. Another grand harvest coming up!

On another subject altogether, I took Uncle Melvin up on his invitation to visit his shop. What a hub of activity. Everything in heaven is custom-made, so I really can't describe anything as being manufactured. However, for lack of a better way to describe it, Uncle Melvin "manufactures" (among other things) some of those hot-plate-like stoves that I described in an earlier letter. He has several guys working with him, guys who are learning the trade. The stoves are made out of a shiny, silverish metal that is unknown on earth. Eight or ten sheets of the metal stood up along the walls of the shop. Uncle Melvin says that he stocks only enough for the orders he has.

I was surprised that someone in heaven would need or want

to learn a trade. Uncle Melvin shrugged. "Do you know all there is to know about music," he asked? "Well, no..." "These fellows were labourers on earth," Uncle Melvin said. "They never had the opportunity to train for anything, but they always dreamed of being sheet metal workers. It was just something that appealed to them. So, here they are. They're learning quickly and they love what they do. In no time at all, they'll be in shops of their own." He showed me around a bit more, and then we hiked down the street for a cup of coffee. Ah ha, this is what you've been waiting for, Mom and Dad, isn't it? For me to discover a coffee shop?

Coffee shops are a very important subject; important enough to begin a new paragraph. Yes, guys, there are coffee shops in heaven and there is coffee, but you'd find both of them somewhat unrecognizable by earth's standards. The coffee shops are little outdoor bistros that serve dainty little fruit cups, fresh vegetable salads, and light pastries made from cornmeal or a wheat-like grain. The coffee smells and tastes exotic, but it is made from a native plant that has no addictive or unhealthy components. This particular coffee shop is run by a bright, friendly young woman whom everybody calls "Honey". The little outdoor "cafe" is right beside her home. I asked her why she did this, and she told me she derived great pleasure from seeing people comfortably visiting together over a cup of coffee and a fruit tart. She felt her cafe was a nice change from "picking it yourself and eating it as is." She's very creative with food but she makes sure that none of the natural flavour is lost. She joined Uncle Melvin and myself for awhile, and then moved on to another table.

Lilli Kehler

Uncle Melvin and I continued to chat . "Do you know why I enjoy this particular coffee shop so much," he asked? I shook my head. "Honey", he said, as though that should explain it all. I waited silently for a long minute and then rose to the bait. "What about Honey? Honey, as in charming? Honey, as in gorgeous, honey-blonde hair? Honey, as in a great chef? What?" He laughed. "See," he said, teasingly, "even in heaven everything is a learning process. You just don't know it all, do you?" I sighed impatiently. Quickly Uncle Melvin became serious. "When Honey was on earth, she was what is commonly known down there as a Downs Syndrome child. She was quite severely mentally handicapped. And yet, look at her today. Isn't she a treasure?" I looked at Honey chatting animatedly with some friends at another table. Suddenly the pieces of the puzzle fell into place, and I understood Uncle Melvin's delight with this girl. I remembered that he has a granddaughter on earth who is a Downs Syndrome child, and he was seeing little Allison, not as she is on earth, but who she will one day become. I felt a thrill shoot through me. No wonder there's no sorrow or tears in heaven. We see things through "heavenly eyes". In other words, we see beyond earth's limitations; we see beyond the pain and the darkness, to the everlasting glory and brightness that is ahead. Oh my, if only earth people could catch that vision! It would help to alleviate so much pain and heartache.

What other loose ends do I have to tie up? I'll just summarize a few odds and ends that I have kind of left hanging in limbo. Nothing very important, but I like to be thorough.

Letters from Heaven

My living room furniture is white and green, a rich, deep green to match that beautiful, emerald table in the hallway of my home. I don't know who picked that table out for me; it was just there when I arrived. We wear simple, but beautifully made, white garments, and we never have to launder them. We don't wear shoes, so Uncle Eddie, you might have to review your career options before you get here. Our bodies and faces, as I mentioned earlier, are recognizable, but are very different from earth bodies in the way they are constructed. The bodies we had on earth were "corruptible", easily broken down, subject to disease and death; our new bodies are "incorruptible", strong, made to last forever. I have attained "super-human" knowledge and wisdom, but when I look around me, I realize there's still so much to learn. Thank God, I have an eternity to learn it in. The babies and children that enter heaven are not given instant maturity, but they grow very rapidly, both in wisdom and in stature. The animals don't talk (aw shucks!), and the water level in the River of Life never rises. There is no rain, but as in the days of the Garden of Eden, we frequently have soft mists that keep everything green and beautiful. Now, that's a pretty fair overview of all the things I have previously left unsaid, isn't it? Incredible as it sounds, anything and everything that I've been able to describe about heaven falls drastically short of the reality. My humble attempts might be compared to those of a young child who patiently draws a simple picture of his house for his kindergarten friends. He knows, and they know, that there's far more to that house than the drawing shows, but showing them the architect's blueprints would be an exercise in futility. They are too immature and too inexperienced to comprehend the complexities of a professional house design. God's heaven is a very complex place. All I have ever wanted to do was give you a shadowy glimpse of the wonderful home that He has prepared for us. It was never my intention to draw you a blueprint.

It's time I came to a close. I think I've said everything I need to say, except, perhaps, for one thing. You and I both know that heaven is not the only place for people to spend eternity. I've been in this paradise for over a year, but that doesn't mean that I have developed amnesia. There is a place called hell, and it was originally prepared for the devil and his angels. Unfortunately, there's a vast number of people out there who haven't clued in to the fact that if they reject Jesus Christ on earth, God will not allow them into His heaven. What, then, is the alternative? Hell! Eternal fire! Eternal darkness! Eternal separation! Wailing and gnashing of teeth![10] Does this sound like the kind of place where anyone would want to spend eternity?

Jesus says, "I am the Way, the Truth and the Life; no one comes to the Father **but by Me**."[11] There is only one way to heaven, and that's through Jesus Christ. People are fooling themselves if they think there are "many roads to God." In this past year, I haven't met one person who got here because of his good works, his brand of religion, or his tolerant attitude. We are all here because each of us, at one time or another while we were still on earth, accepted Jesus Christ as our personal Saviour. We acknowledged that He died for our sins, and that only through His shed blood on the cross could we have eternal life. Eternal life for many of us came much more quickly than we ever thought possible. I didn't expect to be killed in a bizarre motorcycle accident at the age of 21, but thank God, young as I was, I was ready to go. I know you know all this, Mom, Dad and Holly. I'm not telling you anything new. I also know that the three of you are ready to go should the Lord call you. But there are others out there who aren't. Please...go and tell them. Share the wonders of heaven and the bleakness of hell. Remind them that eternity is forever!

I love the three of you. I want to close with the words of a song that I wrote when I was still on earth. "Though the mountains be shaken, and the hills be removed; still God's love will always be there, and His ways will be true." When I wrote those words, I firmly believed them. Now I am fully experiencing His love and His ways, and there is no place else I'd rather be than in His presence - forever! Goodbye, my dear family, and may God's peace and love sustain you until we're all together again.

With all my love, Jay

Lilli Kehler

BIBLICAL REFERENCES:

[1] I Corinthians 13: 12

[2] I Corinthians 13: 13

[3] Romans 8: 38, 39

[4] I Corinthians 2: 9

[5] II Peter 3: 9

[6] Philippians 4: 7

[7] I Thessalonians 5: 18

[8] Matthew 18: 3

[9] Lamentations 3: 22, 23

[10] Matthew 25: 30

[11] John 14: 6

WORSHIP AND PRAISE SONGS

Words & Music by Jay Kehler
Copyright 1993

<u>Though the Mountains</u>

Though the mountains be shaken,
And the hills be removed,
Still your love will always be there
And your ways will be true.

Chorus:

Worthy, you are worthy of my praise,
Your blood has saved me, and I am free,
Glory, I give glory to your name,
Forever I am yours,
And forever will my praises be.

Like the rain falls on the dry ground
And brings life to the rose,
So your love will fall upon me
'Til my heart overflows.

Repeat Chorus:

Lord, I Want to Be a Sacrifice

Lord, I want to be a sacrifice,
Lord, I want to be pleasing to you,
Lord, I want your love to rule my life
And be the one, that you shine through.

Chorus:

Jesus, I give you all,
Every part of me cries out your name,
Jesus, I give you all,
Living and holy,
Living and holy,
Living and holy...for you.

No Love Like Yours

Oh Lord my God, who is like you?
You rule the earth and sea,
Yet you live inside of me.
Oh Lord my God, who is like you?
You looked down upon my life,
Yet you chose to pay my price.

Chorus:

And I'll sing praise to you, all my days,
Lord, you are so precious to me,
Your sweet grace came and took my place,
Oh my Lord, there is no love like yours.

Oh Lord my God, who is like you?
I give you all my pain,
And you give me joy again.
Oh Lord my God, who is like you?
You're crowned with majesty...
I come to you on bended knee.

Repeat Chorus: